THE TITANIC
DIARIES

Anthony Cunningham worked in the Education Department at Hampton Court Palace before becoming a teacher. *The Titanic Diaries* is his first book.

THE TITANIC DIARIES

Dramatic accounts of shipwreck survival

Anthony Cunningham

• A SILVER LINK BOOK •

from

The NOSTALGIA Collection

To Edith Maud Rogers –
Who always believed in me

© Anthony Cunningham 2005

First published in 2005

British Library Cataloguing in Publication Data

A catalogue record for this book is available from the British Library.

ISBN 1 85794 231 0

Silver Link Publishing Ltd
The Trundle
Ringstead Road
Great Addington
Kettering
Northants NN14 4BW

Tel/Fax: 01536 330588
email: sales@nostalgiacollection.com
Website: www.nostalgiacollection.com

Printed and bound in Great Britain

The quotation from *Testament of Youth* by Vera Brittain is included by permission of Mark Bostridge and Rebecca Williams, her literary executors, as well as Victor Gollancz, a division of the Orion Publishing Group, as the publisher.

CONTENTS

FOREWORD

by Pat Lacey
Great great niece of *Titanic*'s Captain Edward Smith

It was a great pleasure and privilege to be asked to write a Foreword for this excellent diary.

Anthony Cunningham has collected a host of personal narratives from shipwreck survivors that otherwise may never have been put into print. For that, we owe him a debt of gratitude. Stories like these are so often passed down within families from one generation to the next, but never committed to paper. Many are lost for ever. How I wish I could turn back the hands of time so that I could ask my relatives more about Uncle Edward!

Edward John Smith is famous to any maritime enthusiast as being Captain Smith, master of the *Titanic*. Sadly, I never knew him because he was killed when the liner sank on 15 April 1912. However, he was considered a hero in the family and was the subject of many a conversation. Since his calling was considered more appropriate to a boy than to a girl, the photograph of Uncle Edward, the handsome, bearded sailor in the uniform of the White Star Line, always hung upon the wall of my brother's bedroom. I was given the slim volume of verse inscribed in a clear and precise hand: 'To Edward J. Smith from his mother, on his 10th birthday'. That, at least, is how I remember it, since I was foolish enough to lend out the book and not to ensure its return – an oversight that I was later to regret deeply.

In true naval tradition Captain Smith went down with his ship. One witness was positive that he saw the captain saving a baby while swimming over to the upturned lifeboat B – a version certainly believed by his wife. *Titanic* scholars have put forward convincing arguments that he was on the bridge as the sea water crashed in around him. His last words were said to be, 'Be British!' – a fine piece of Edwardian rhetoric – but we shall never be sure. This is how I imagined the scene in my novelised biography:

'...the deck chairs that people, even now, were throwing into the sea as makeshift rafts, and doors wrenched from their hinges – rained down around his shoulders as he trod water, desperately trying to stay afloat in the massive swell, so that he could go down, if not upon the *Titanic*, at least with her. A chair hit his shoulder, another his arm, and

7

another... It was only a glancing blow to the head, but it was sufficient. He drifted into unconsciousness...'

Reading *The Titanic Diaries* has been an education in the way people react when faced with disasters at sea. I have found the book to be a most compelling read and feel certain that you will share in my enthusiasm.

INTRODUCTION

'Hold me up in mighty waters,
Keep my eyes on things above...'
Autumn, Louis Von Esch

When I was a little boy in the late 1970s I can remember going to the small local library and asking for a book about the *Titanic*. The motherly librarian picked out a well-thumbed illustrated edition of Walter Lord's *A Night to Remember* for me. I found a quiet, sunny corner, and started flicking through the pages.

Those pictures *fascinated* me. How could such beautiful rooms have existed on a ship? And how extraordinary it was to my juvenile mind that they were now enveloped in gloomy darkness on the ocean floor. I wondered what the Cafe Parisien looked like; no doubt the delicate wicker tables and chairs were jumbled up in a corner, here some dainty china cups and saucers in a splintered heap, there a light bulb suspended by a frayed and knotty wire... The hands on the clock mounted beneath the dome of the first class staircase, frozen at 2.20am... And the ghosts. My childish imagination pictured them mournfully gliding through indigo shrouded lounges and decks searching, searching for just one more lifeboat to take them back to the living...

Grainy black and white photographs of the survivors caught my eye. What had the reality of it been like for them? How did it feel to be on that sinking ship in the middle of a vast and lonely sea?

Twenty years later some of those questions were answered for me by a very special lady, *Titanic* survivor Millvina Dean. When I got home I wrote up the visit in my diary. It had been a wonderful day and I didn't want it to pass unremarked. Millvina also let me record her memories on tape so I pasted in the transcript too as a precious keepsake.

That got me thinking about other shipwrecks. How was it for those people who survived disasters at sea such as the *Lusitania*, *Eastland*, *Morro Castle* and *Lancastria* – to name but a few? What were 'their Titanic' stories like? For example, I wanted to know what it was like to heed the call of those dreadful words, 'Abandon Ship!' What choices do you have to make when you're in a life and death situation like that? How do you *live* with a shipwreck in your life? Do you learn to cope and put the memory of it to one side, or does it not affect you at all? Is the euphoria of salvation quickly swamped by sensations of grief, horror, shame? In September 1999 I began tracing living survivors of shipping disasters and noted everything down along the way in what I came to refer to as my 'Titanic Diary'. Little did I know then that it was going to last five years!

Many of the shipwreck survivors I spoke with allude to or compare their experience with the *Titanic*. Some note with sadness that the public obsession with the *Titanic* has pushed their ship into the margins of history. It gradually became clear to me that people habitually tend to regard the *Titanic* disaster as a kind of 'benchmark' with which we compare subsequent calamities at sea. Other maritime disasters, it seems, are juxtaposed with the 'ship of dreams' – and found wanting.

I've always been curious about the legacy of the *Titanic* disaster, so I set out to find a few of the children and close relatives of those who perished and of those who survived, to see what effect it had on them. After all, it can't be easy growing up with such a legend as part of the family, can it? Rather like having Elvis as a permanent guest in the back bedroom and the world camped outside with its nose pressed against the window and ear to the door.

However, occasionally the *Titanic* popped into my life unexpectedly like a pantomime demon sprung from a trap. Now and then it was even comical. Therefore the theme recurs in these pages, weaving its way through the text. Eventually I came to adopt a name for these entries – 'Titanic threads'.

As we turn the corner of a new century the *Titanic* has, unsurprisingly, also become a historic signpost marking out a long life. My mother works in a day centre for the elderly and over the years I have met quite a few nonagenarians and centenarians who all seem to take pride in the fact that they can 'remember when the *Titanic* went down'. In February 2005 my local newspaper printed a picture of an old lady on the front cover. The headline was 'Titanic Remembered'. Turning to the relevant page, I found that Mrs Winifred Randall had reached her 100th birthday and her daughter had thrown her a party. The *Titanic* link was brief:

> 'One of her earliest memories is of the day the *Titanic* sank and how all the neighbours stood at her back gate in Ealing talking about the disaster. She was seven at the time the liner went down.'

Winifred Randall had lived through two World Wars, yet this was barely mentioned. None the less, I caught myself thinking, 'How amazing! Here's someone who heard the news as it happened.' So it doesn't seem to matter how thin the connection, 93 years after the *Titanic* sank she can still dominate the headlines.

Like the tide, the *Titanic* may recede now and then from view, but she always returns. You could argue that ever since 1912 she has been the greatest survivor of them all.

In the heave and swell of history the *Titanic* saturates every other shipwreck in her wake. However, no one could fail to be touched by Holis Pifer's tale of the *San Juan* or Adella Leibenow Wotherspoon and the sorry saga of the *General Slocum*. Consider for a moment the fortitude of Ronald Thomas and George Crow during (and after) the attack on the *Empress of Asia*. Millvina Dean's childhood *Titanic* reminiscences find parallels in those of Audrey Pearl and Barbara Anderson on the *Lusitania* in 1915. Lawrence Beesley is the famous teacher in the *Titanic* story, but at least he left his work at home; there was no such respite for Kathleen Preston on board the doomed *Empress of Britain*.

Every *Titanic* buff can tell you about the heroes made when the ship went down, but they find their equal in the bravery of Colin Ryder Richardson, John Vass Morris, Leonard Jones, Ken Belsham and Ivor Thomas ... the list goes on. The courage of the women manning the oars on that mill-pond sea during the *Titanic* disaster was thought extraordinary at the time. But after jumping in a lifeboat as the *Athenia* sank, Ceinwen Preddy found herself up to her knees in freezing-cold water and with only a fifty-fifty chance of rescue. Roy Leadbetter appreciates more than most how the *Titanic*'s remaining passengers felt when the ship left them thrashing about on the surface of the Atlantic. He still shivers at the memory of dropping off the *Rawalpindi*'s stern rail into the sea in November 1939.

Film star Dorothy Gibson was one of the celebrated beauties on board the *Titanic*, but just take a look at Dolly Davidson McTigue from the *Morro Castle* – she could have given Ginger Rogers a run for her money. As for Elizabeth Dunn and Audrey Tiller, they're like a couple of Gainsborough starlets.

The *Titanic* became infamous for its lack of lifeboats – something the passengers on board the fire-ravaged *Lakonia* could relate to on her maiden voyage in 1963 when many of their lifeboats were rendered unusable. Even the pathos of those immigrants on the *Titanic* aspiring for a better life in the New World is mirrored in Pierette Simpson's account of the *Andrea Doria* disaster in 1956.

In the past five years I have been fortunate enough to meet with dozens of survivors so that I could hear their stories first hand. I spoke to nearly all of the contributors on the telephone during that time, hastily making scribbled notes along the way. When asked to do so, people haven't hesitated in taping their oral histories, while a few preferred to e-mail or to write them down for me. Complete strangers have sent me extracts from private memoirs, correspondence and newspaper clippings. One unforeseen and welcome enrichment of my life concerning this diary has been the formation of lasting friendships with survivors both at home and abroad.

Sometimes I would find myself blithely typing up a transcript without really taking in the words when suddenly a phrase would jump out at me and bring me up short. Each number in those statistics is a *life* – a man, woman or child. Here is the human spirit at one with the sea in the most literal and awesome circumstances. Gives you pause for thought, doesn't it?

'I thought I was entering paradise, for I was alive and about to breathe again, and then I heard the cries of souls in torment and believed myself in hell. Dear God! Those voices! *Father... Father...For the love of Christ... Help me, for pity's sake!... Where is my son?* Some called for their mothers, some on the Lord, some to die quickly, a few to be saved. The lamentations rang through the frosty air and touched the stars... Then silence fell, and that was the worst sound of all.'

Every Man for Himself, Beryl Bainbridge

TITANIC
(1912)

9 September 1999

It's not every day you get to meet a *Titanic* survivor is it? Today I did. L. and I had been invited for afternoon tea and as we drove down to Southampton in the baking sun I was nervous and tense. I don't think I could have been more jittery if I'd been invited to Clarence House for an audience with the Queen Mother. I fiddled with my tie. Madness to be so overdressed in this weather! It's just that I felt so honoured to be in such company. I was perspiring and I knew it wasn't just the heat. It was a childlike, burning anticipation.

Millvina's home is considerably smaller than Clarence House. In fact it's a very modest bungalow with a pretty garden. But it's filled with laughter and good will. It was a good job I asked if I could record her memories on my tape recorder as most of the afternoon I sat there just watching her – watching this woman who had been on the *Titanic* for its one and only voyage. Look at any photograph of the *Titanic* leaving Southampton. *Millvina Dean was on it*. Somewhere in that leviathan was a little girl heading straight for the history books.

The sinking of the *Titanic* remains one of the most resonant stories of disaster at sea. Every year the public appetite for this tragedy is fed with more books, periodicals, documentaries, radio programmes, films and even musicals than any other maritime disaster. As a little boy it fascinated me. It still does. The question is, why?

Even Dr Robert Ballard, who in 1985 discovered the wreck, found it hard to analyse:

'When I first thought about looking for the *Titanic*, the ship represented little more than a technological challenge... However, the more familiar I became with her story, the more my fascination grew. Soon this grand old lady of the deep had me completely in her spell... By rights she should have been dead and buried long since. Yet her allure seems greater today than ever.'

Walter Lord offers us an explanation in the illustrated edition of his account of the disaster, *A Night to Remember*:

'The appeal seems universal. To social historians it is a microcosm of the early 1900s. To nautical enthusiasts it is the ultimate shipwreck. To students of human nature it is an endlessly fascinating laboratory. For lovers of nostalgia it has the allure of yesterday. For day-dreamers, it has all those might have beens.'

Millvina Dean is the youngest survivor of the disaster. She put it concisely enough this afternoon: 'The *Titanic* story will never die.' Indeed, the *Titanic* appears to be as much of our time as the public who marvelled at her scale and mourned her loss back in 1912. It seems her legend is simply part of modern folklore.

Commissioned as the largest ship in the world and fitted with innovative safety features and luxurious appointments, the *Titanic* was a stunning addition to the White Star Line. Though it was never claimed by her owners, there was a popular myth spread abroad that she was unsinkable.

The *Titanic* left from Southampton on her maiden voyage bound for New York on 10 April 1912 with approximately 2,203 passengers and crew. Four days later, on a calm, starlit night, she collided with an iceberg and sank in just over two hours. Tragically, the loss of life was increased by a serious shortage of lifeboats. Only 705 people survived to complete their journey.

When I contacted Millvina Dean I couldn't help wondering what she would be like. Would she care to discuss the disaster, having done so many, *many* times before? I need not have worried. Her kindness to strangers is genuine. Her evident humility at receiving so much attention is touching. Wherever she and the handful of remaining *Titanic* survivors go, crowds flock to see them. Deluged with requests for public appearances, interviews, autographs, book signings … they are 'Titanic Ambassadors', memorial guardians of that 'grand old lady of the deep'. Millvina Dean said today, 'People tell me I'm like living history.' She is indeed.

MILLVINA DEAN

❝ We weren't supposed to go on the *Titanic* originally. We had been booked onto another ship called the *Philadelphia*, but there was a coal strike at the time and all the fuel had to be taken off the smaller ships so that the *Titanic* could make its maiden voyage. The White Star Line got in touch with my father and asked him if he would like to change his booking – would he like to go on the *Titanic*? And he agreed straight away. He was so excited because everyone had heard about the *Titanic*. My grandfather, who had come to see us off said, 'You'll have a wonderful time. It's a beautiful ship.'

We had to travel in steerage [third class] because it was so expensive. We were emigrating to Kansas. My father was a publican but he wanted to start a tobacconist shop in America. So they sold everything to get the fare and saved what money they could. My mother was terribly brave undertaking a journey like that, with my brother Bertram and I being so young. She did manage to send a postcard off to my grandmother from the ship saying that everything was fine – just a couple of lines because she can't have had much spare time. I also remember her saying there was a band of some kind in the third class which she enjoyed listening to but she didn't say much about the voyage in general – she couldn't bear to think about it. In fact, it wasn't until years later that my mother told me about what happened on the night.

Bertram and I were, naturally, fast asleep in bed. My father heard something was amiss and said he would go up on deck to find out what happened. He hadn't been gone long when he rushed into the cabin and said, 'There's been a crash – the ship has hit an iceberg. Get the children out of bed and up on deck as quickly as possible and make sure they're wearing something warm.' So my mother dressed us as best she could and we made our way to the lifeboats.

The most dreadful thing happened as my mother and I were put into a boat. Somehow Bertram toddled off. My mother didn't know where he was and there was nothing she could do because she had me in her arms. They had to lower the lifeboat into the water without him. It was bad enough without her husband beside her but to know that your son had gone too must have been dreadful. She must have been sick with worry.

Apparently, while we were in the lifeboat a woman got hysterical and started saying over and over that she had lost her feather bed. It didn't matter that her husband had just died, all she was concerned about was her feather bed! I suppose she must have been in shock. They also picked up a Chinese man who was floating on a raft of some kind. The other women didn't want to take him in saying that it was disgusting that he should have lived while their husbands were dead. Thankfully they thought better of it. 'Heroism and chivalry are the great myths about the Titanic,' my mother said. 'This might have true somewhere on the boat deck. But really, it was arrogance and madness that night … madness.'

We didn't know what had become of Bertram until we were rescued by the *Carpathia* in the morning. Another passenger had put him into a lifeboat – so whoever did that saved his life. Someone else had taken care of him until he was handed back to my mother. She must have been overwhelmed and I suppose she always hoped her husband would turn up too but, of course, he never did. We couldn't possibly stay in America without my father so after a few weeks spent recuperating in St Luke's Hospital in New York we came home.

We returned to England on the *Adriatic* and when we arrived in Liverpool the press were waiting to meet the survivors. That's when I was photographed in my mother's arms. They called me a 'Loveable mite of humanity' because I was the youngest survivor of the disaster. I was passed around the other passengers like a lucky charm! I still have the original 1912 newspaper clipping of it somewhere.

After we came home we were helped my the Titanic Relief Fund. My mother got a pension and our schooling was paid for until Bertram and I were eighteen. That was the only connection we ever had with the *Titanic*. My mother had no interest in it apart from our education. I never even *knew* that I had been on the *Titanic* until I was eight years old. My mother was getting remarried and decided to tell me. I didn't know anything about it before then and it didn't mean a thing to me.

I was a highly strung child. Subconsciously I think it must have been to do with the *Titanic* – with my mother breast-feeding me on the ship and being a mass of nerves. It must have affected me in my early years. I was very good at school, ever such a bright child. I wasn't used to getting into trouble and if I ever did for some reason I would burst into tears. I was never treated any differently from the other children because of the *Titanic* and as far as I know I was the only child there who had lost a parent on the ship.

My mother lived until she was 96 yet she rarely ever talked about the *Titanic* or my father. I suppose it was because she had remarried and it would have been awkward. She never wrote about it either and as far as I know never gave any interviews – she just couldn't bear to think about it. The furthest she would go on a boat after the *Titanic* disaster was to the Isle of Wight.

She did keep some things from that night on the ship, though, like the little coat, booties and a blanket that I had been wearing that night. However, they all got moth-eaten and had to be thrown away. They were kept in an old trunk for years and Bertram and I only found them after she died.

It never entered my mind to miss my father. My grandfather was a substitute father to me. My stepfather was a kind man but no replacement for my grandfather. However, when I look back, it was clear that he liked children. He was very good with Bertram and me. My brother was a bit scared of him, I think, because if he wanted anything from him, he'd ask me to ask him! I was the one who always had to step forward on his behalf. But I think that my stepfather coped very well really under the circumstances.

I didn't have any ambitions at all as I grew up. I stayed at home because my stepfather was a vet and we had a large house with stables. There was so much work to do with all the animals. I was there until the Second World War when I was called up. I went into the Ordnance Survey Office drawing maps and spent the entire war doing that. I enjoyed it very much there and I made the best friends I ever had. Everybody was frightened during the war and yet they were some of my happiest days. You could walk home in the blackout and you always felt safe. I really wasn't interested in a career. After the war I didn't even want to stay in the Ordnance Survey Office so I worked in the purchasing department of an engineering firm in Hampshire.

The *Titanic* had absolutely no effect on my life whatsoever until the wreck was found in 1985. Up until then no one knew about me and I never gave the *Titanic* a second thought. Then the American Titanic Society realised who I was and wanted to interview me. I haven't stopped since!

I like people, which is very handy because I now do a lot of travelling and meet people from all over the world. It's fascinating. I like everybody – whether they're high or low, they're OK with me. That's really the best part about it.

I've also had quite a lot of contact with other survivors over the years – particularly with two of our English ones – Eva Hart and Edith Haisman. I've met a French survivor, Michel Navratil, but of course he doesn't speak a word of English and my French is non-existent, so the conversation was limited! While I was in Paris at a *Titanic*-related event, I met Louise Laroche and you should have seen her – she was a tiny woman! I felt like a giant next to her. She was about the smallest person I have ever seen. She was a dear little one, even though she didn't enjoy the publicity much. I've met American survivors too and a Swedish lady called Beatrice Sandstrom.

Whenever I meet survivors we never have time to talk to each other – ever! We just say, 'Hello, how are you?' And that's the end of it because there are always plenty of photographers and people who want interviews and autographs. When I first went to America I hardly had time to eat or drink. I was completely surrounded all the time. Even a reporter from the *New York Times* came down to see me and he was a horrible, arrogant little man. He didn't like me and I certainly didn't like him. He strutted in and everyone said, 'Oh, the *New York Times* is like that, they think they're the cat's whiskers.' Unbelievable. I must admit, last year [1998] I was fed up with the *Titanic* because of the film [James Cameron's *Titanic*]. Everybody kept phoning me wanting me to give radio interviews, make special appearances and so forth. They were contacting me from all over the world. I got absolutely tired of the whole thing. But now it's eased down a bit. Last year I was away for part of every month to America, Germany, Switzerland, opening all sorts of exhibitions. People are so kind, though. They always make a big fuss of me so, of course, I love it most of the time.

In 1997 I was invited to travel on the *QE2* to complete my journey to Kansas, which I should have done all those years ago in 1912 on the *Titanic*. When I arrived I was taken to see the house which I would have lived in. There was a huge crowd of people outside, and I said, 'Look at all my relations!' Well, there turned out to be only one solitary relation of mine there – and he was so shy he hardly said anything! They were so charming the people I met there. I had champagne when I arrived, cakes and things, and then they took me to see the nursery where I would have been taken as a baby. That was really creepy. They asked me if I would have liked to have lived in Kansas and I said, 'Of course – but I wouldn't have known anything else to compare it with.' Just imagine, for all those early years I wasn't the slightest bit interested in the *Titanic*. I think I must have been a rather weird child because I never asked anyone about it – not a thing. I didn't even want to know about my real father. I look back now and think it odd but at the time it seemed natural. Bertram was far more interested in it than me and he did a lot of research about the ship. He died a few years ago on the anniversary of the sinking, which everybody thought was quite strange – an extraordinary coincidence, in fact.

I went to see the film version of *A Night to Remember* many, many years ago. That was the only thing I ever did that was *Titanic*-related before 1985. I saw it with about four or five other survivors in Boston and we all hated it because our fathers had been killed on the ship. It was a dreadful experience. We were absolutely appalled. One person said she had nightmares for weeks afterwards and that we should never had been taken to see it and I agree. I couldn't help thinking all the while about my poor father. I've never seen the film since and I don't want to see anything like that again. I haven't seen the latest film either, even though people have invited me to private screenings. I couldn't bear to see those scenes re-enacted.

However, I have been to a number of events recreating the last dinner on board the *Titanic*. It's all done as if you're in first class so I suppose you could say after eighty-eight years my ticket has been upgraded! We dress in 1912 clothes, which is rather lovely. But the first one I went to in Canada was strange because I hardly had anything to eat. It was amazing. From the minute I sat down at the table dozens of young men came up to me saying, 'I must catch you now Millvina because there'll be no time after', and they didn't stop talking. All the while I could see this beautiful food being taken away and the next course arriving and I could only take the odd mouthful.

I'm always completely surrounded by people all the time, asking me questions. I was guest of honour at a *Titanic* function once and I have to tell you it was terribly embarrassing. As I walked out into the huge dining room absolutely everyone started clapping. I practically ran to my seat!

I'm often asked to open museum exhibitions about the *Titanic* but I rarely ever get to actually see anything because of everyone wanting autographs and so on. Still, people are always very polite – although one or two get a bit over-excited now and then. One woman I met at a convention burst into tears in front of me because she couldn't believe she'd met a survivor. All I could do was pat her on the arm saying, 'There, there, dear, calm down.' It was strange. I'm sometimes asked to do signing sessions of prints and photographs and you have to concentrate very carefully. I once started writing out my address on a print by mistake, instead of my name, but no one seemed to mind. They said it added interest!

Although I adore going on the *QE2* and other fine ships I don't believe in these proposals to build replicas of the *Titanic* for commercial use today. I don't think they should rebuild a tragedy. No. *One Titanic* was enough.

CITY OF BENARES
(1940)

13 July 2000

Colin Ryder Richardson still finds it painful to talk about the *City of Benares* disaster. As he told me himself yesterday afternoon, 'It changed everything for me, more so than perhaps I realised at the time and not for the better.' Looking at him in that moment I saw how difficult it can be for people to open up and trawl deep into their past. A modest, unassuming man, he did not even tell me that because of his courage during the disaster he became the youngest person to be awarded the King's Commendation for Brave Conduct in the Merchant Navy. The Dictaphone purred away and he told me the whole sorry story.

With the fall of France in June 1940 a flood of invitations from the dominions calling for children to be sent abroad put the Government headed by Winston Churchill in something of a quandary. Churchill commanded MP Geoffrey Shakespeare to oversee the matter and chair a committee to look into the feasibility of the idea of sending children further afield. Shakespeare established the Children's Overseas Reception Board (CORB), whose criteria finally met with Cabinet approval on 17 June 1940, despite grave personal reservations by the PM.

After a number of advertisements and radio broadcasts, the scheme received in excess of 200,000 applications. The response was so overwhelming that the whole operation was closed down after only two weeks. This, however, did not stop parents who were willing to send their children away on privately based schemes. Between July and September 1940 an estimated 3,100 children were sent to Commonwealth countries such as Australia, Canada, New Zealand and South Africa.

What most people did not realise was that due to lack of resources the British Admiralty could not guarantee the 'seavacuees' a naval escort for the entire duration of their journey. In addition, mothers and fathers were asked to sign an indemnity form discharging the Government of any responsibility for their children's protection at sea. Fearing the worst on the home front, what could they do but agree to the terms and hope for the best?

Owned by the Ellerman Line of Great Britain and designed as a single-class ship, the *City of Benares* had served the Liverpool to Bombay route before the outbreak of hostilities. On 13 September 1940 it joined convoy OB213 bound for Montreal and Quebec, carrying more than 400 passengers and crew, including 99 'seavacuees'.

On 17 September she was torpedoed twice on the port side by U-boat U-48 under the command of Kapitanleutnant Heinrich Bleichrodt. Only 256 people survived the attack. That night 77 children perished in the tempestuous North Atlantic. Ironically, the naval escort had departed a mere 21 hours before. Many of the lifeboats launched capsized due to the inclement weather, drowning their occupants, while the remaining passengers and crew found themselves badly exposed to the elements in boats that were, in some cases, unseaworthy. The following day HMS *Hurricane* picked up the bulk of those survivors still living, but one boat drifted on the open sea for ten days before rescue appeared.

COLIN RYDER RICHARDSON

66 There was a very real threat of a full-scale German invasion after the fall of France in June 1940, so my parents decided it would be safer to send me overseas. My father was a lawyer and a number of QCs in New York had formed some sort of organisation whereby they would take the children of British lawyers as evacuees. It was arranged that I would go to America and stay with a family there.

We were living in Monmouthshire at the time, having already moved out of London because of the bombing raids. I was terribly excited to be going away and didn't really think about the implications of not seeing my parents for what could have been years. As an eleven-year-old boy you only see what is in front of you and not the long term. You don't stop to analyse the situation. Besides, my mother had a terrific confidence in the Royal Navy and told me that if anything happened they would make sure we were rescued.

I'd never been on a ship before, so that was a new experience for me. My mother accompanied me to Liverpool docks where I was to board the ship. My father was working in London so he couldn't come. Later on my mother told me I hardly even waved her goodbye at the terminal – I suppose I was too caught up in the excitement of it all. The ship looked huge to me and I think it was painted an orange/pink colour. My mother had given me a bright red lifejacket to wear and told me that as soon as the ship left the harbour I was to put it on and not take it off. It was rather like a coat, in fact, and very practical for a transatlantic crossing because it kept me nice and warm out on deck. I must have stood out in the crowd because very quickly the other passengers nicknamed me 'Will Scarlet'!

We were escorted on board by the crew and at once I noticed that they were in fact Indian sailors – or Laskers as they were properly called. I was taken into a reception room and then hustled off to my cabin. I was sharing my room with an adult passenger, a Mr Raski, who was a Hungarian journalist. He didn't speak much English and I hardly saw him at all during the voyage. Later on, however, he saved my life.

For me, being on the *City of Benares* was rather like a school outing – a sort of adventure camp. I didn't see much of the CORB evacuees during the trip and I think they had lessons during the day. I spent most of my time alone, although I can remember palling up with a few children now and then. We used to have fun playing with deckchairs once we got out to sea because we discovered that the wind was strong enough on deck to move the chairs from one side of the promenade to the other. It was also an endless source of interest watching the rest of the convoy, but then it left us after a few days.

The ship had a nice library which I used quite a bit – I was a big reader – but most of all I enjoyed the food, which was quite wonderful. The meals seemed rather exotic to me, especially after the austerity of rationing in Britain. I can recall having curry (which I didn't much like) and delicious desserts. In England we used to have National Loaf which was very brown and not that tasty. Being aboard a luxury passenger liner was simply heaven after having been denied interesting food for so long! The ship wasn't as splendid or glamorous as the *Queen Mary* or *Olympic*, but to a young eleven-year-old it seemed very stately – lots of wood panelling and chic furniture. My cabin was charming with a handsome armoire and two beds made up with crisp linen. During the trip I put a ball-bearing in the top drawer of my bedside cabinet so that I could hear how rough or calm the weather was. I can remember it going CLINK, CLINK, CLINK against the wood.

We waited for a day at the entrance of the River Mersey in order for the convoy to assemble, so I spent my first night at sea just outside Liverpool. The convoy had to go slowly because there were about thirty ships altogether – some of them quite small. The *City of Benares* was the commodore ship and it led the convoy – we had the admiral of the fleet on board to oversee the crossing. On the stern of the ship there was a huge gun mounted, which the Laskers practised on during the voyage. I suppose that gun was reason enough for the U-boat to sink us, being 'armed' as we were. Luckily I never got seasick, which was a relief. There was a lifeboat drill on the first Sunday. We had only been at sea two days. First of all you had to go to your lifeboat station, which for me was in the reception room. Then you were assigned your lifeboat under escort – mine was number 6, the third one along on the starboard side. After that we had a religious service. You also had to wear the regulation lifejacket, but since I already had the one mother gave me I felt rather restricted putting this other one on top. It was a bulky thing made of cork. Instead, I used to drag mine around with me all over the place.

I never really gave the idea of being torpedoed a great deal of thought until it actually happened. I figured it was a lot safer being on the ship than being bombed back in England. However, I read the newspapers and even at that age I knew what was going on. Every day you would read about the Germans getting closer and closer, the fall of Dunkirk and so on. To be perfectly honest I was much more excited about the prospect of being in New York (having thoughts of Hollywood in my mind) than thinking about the danger. It was all such an adventure.

On the actual night of the sinking I was reading my comic in bed. Suddenly there was a large bang, which shook the whole ship. The most distinctive thing I remember, however, was the smell of cordite, which is unmistakable. If you have ever played with a pop gun you'll know. It's rather like nail varnish – a singular smell. I didn't know exactly what had happened but I knew there had been an explosion of some sort. I got up and spent a couple of minutes wondering if I should put my lifejacket on first or my dressing-gown. In the end I had to go back for my slippers because I forgot them. I made my way to the reception area where it was pretty chaotic. People were asking, 'What's going on?' I didn't say anything because the adults wouldn't have been interested in the ramblings of a little boy, but I listened to what they were saying. There seemed to be no immediate rush for the lifeboats at this point because there was a possibility that we wouldn't have to abandon ship. Other ships had survived being torpedoed so it wasn't as crazy as it sounds.

Then sure enough the instruction to make for the lifeboats came and there was concerted movement – not a panic as such but no one was sticking around! The CORB children all came streaming up with their minders too, and at that point Mr Raski appeared. The ship wasn't listing much then but there was a problem getting into the lifeboat because there was a gale blowing and the boats were swinging wildly against the ship's hull leaving a gap. You had to wait until the boat swung near enough to the deck and then jump for it. The call came for women first so that they could help the children on. Mr Raski was there to help me and would have got in the boat himself but stepped back to let other women on. He never made it.

There was a full moon and the ship's lights were ablaze but the weather was rough. In the end there were about forty people in the boat. I suddenly realised how cold I was and this was exacerbated by the spray coming from the sea. I was sat next to an elderly nurse whom I held on to.

As soon as we hit the water we were in trouble. The boat wasn't seaworthy and flooded straight away. Obviously no one had checked if the wood was sound and I suppose it had shrunk having been in the tropical sunshine. There we were sat in the boat with water up to our chests. It was almost like sitting in a bath. I lost my dressing-gown and had to hold on for dear life because my lifejacket was making me buoyant – every wave that hit the boat threatened to dislocate me from my seat. The ship's carpenter was also in the boat and he tried bailing it out but it was no good. The only thing keeping us afloat were two air tanks at the bow and stern.

We tried to row get away from the ship because we were afraid of the suction pulling us down with it. The rudder of our lifeboat had floated away with the oars and the manually operated propeller wouldn't work. By now the *Benares* was sinking stern-first. You could see the portholes slowly going under the water and the lights were all still burning as the ship sank. There was also oil spewing into the sea, making the waves less ferocious but covering us in the lifeboat at the same time, which wasn't very pleasant. The poor nurse was terribly fretful and I spent most of my time trying to comfort her and the other passengers. I had a blind faith that rescue would come.

All around us there were people screaming and crying out. You couldn't speak much because every time you opened your mouth you got a mouth full of seawater in it. I was trying to keep my feet on a tin under my seat, which appeared to be food in case we needed it later. We were filled to capacity but still people came swimming over to us asking to get in, but we couldn't take them – it was impossible.

Rescue took a long time coming. We went in the sea at about 10 o'clock and were picked up by the HMS *Hurricane* at 4 o'clock the next afternoon – about twenty hours. The trouble with being in the water that long is that your fingers go all soft and your bones stiffen up. It was dreadfully cold and all night people were just dying all around me. One student in this mid-twenties went a bit mad and started drinking seawater. By the morning he was foaming at the mouth. Eventually he simply drifted overboard – there was nothing we could do to stop him.

The saddest thing was seeing the nurse die. She must have had a heart attack and she just slumped into my arms. The other people in the boat were saying, 'Let her go', but I couldn't – it was heartbreaking. I had told her to hang on and wait because I was sure we would be rescued but she simply gave up. Eventually the screams died away and by the afternoon it was pretty quiet. We heard that the other evacuee ship had also been torpedoed and for some reason I thought that they would help us, but I suppose they couldn't have even if they wanted to.

By the time the *Hurricane* arrived there were only about six people still alive in the boat. The crew threw down nets for us to climb aboard but we couldn't grip anything. In the end they lifted us up on winches. We were taken into the engine room to warm up. The crew were so young – the captain was only about twenty-four! When I see them now at reunions they don't seem much older than me. Anyway, they treated us with great kindness, giving us clothes to wear and so forth.

We were brought back to Greenock in Scotland where, unbelievably, a port official demanded to see our passports before he would let us in! Of course we didn't have a thing with us, and eventually they let us through to the terminal. No one seemed to know what to do with us and we were shuffled around until we ended up in a hotel. I can remember walking into the lobby in my pyjamas and nobody batted an eyelid – it was as if it were the most normal thing in the world.

Somehow my mother managed to find out where I was, but it had been quite difficult because the disaster hadn't been reported in the national press. When we arrived in Scotland we were photographed and interviewed, but the reporters weren't allowed to release the story until they had the go-ahead from the Government. My mother had to travel all the way up to Scotland when getting around was difficult because of war restrictions. I was overjoyed to see her of course.

The disaster changed my life. I went out a confident well-balanced boy and when I came back I found myself a 'hero' for looking after the nurse. I didn't understand it at all and I felt distanced from the experience and what everyone was saying about me. Psychologically it altered my perceptions completely. My schoolwork suffered and I ended up going into the Navy as a sort of 'fait accompli'. Other survivors can talk about it much more freely because their experiences were different. One boy I know was in a lifeboat that stayed afloat and drifted about without getting waterlogged – for him it was a big adventure. But to me it was horrific and I've never really got over it. I hardly ever talk about the disaster today and only ever think about it seriously when I go to the reunions every ten years. It's something I'd rather had never happened to me, but it's always there.

Titanic threads...
Lawrence Beesley

As a teacher myself I consider Lawrence Beesley to be a kindred spirit. He taught young people on and off for most of his life – notably as a science master at Dulwich College. He was a keen scholar and during his postgraduate research he discovered a rare fountain alga that was named after him – Ulvella Beesleyi.

The 35-year-old Lawrence Beesley boarded the *Titanic* at Southampton on a second class ticket and occupied cabin D56. His daughter Laurien claimed that he was going over to America 'in half-hearted pursuit of an American heiress, whom he hoped to persuade to marry him'. He never did meet his wealthy lady friend. Instead, on landing in New York he was approached by the editor of the *Boston Globe* who asked if he would write a full account of the disaster. After six weeks holed up in a residential club in Boston he finished the manuscript. Called *The Loss of the Titanic*, the book examined the events leading up to and beyond the night of the 14th/15th with a level of moderation in its tone far removed from some of the sensational (and in some cases completely fictional) stories emerging from the press.

Reading Lawrence Beesley's book today it is clear that he did his research most thoroughly. As a scientist used to observing objectively, analysing, recording and commenting, one would expect his story to be rather cold or clinical. Not at all. The *Titanic* was Beesley's first experience of liner travel and he was eager to record each moment and sensation. This short, lyrical extract highlights just how moved he was by the poetry he found in the days preceding the disaster:

'And each night the sun sank right in our eyes along the sea, marking an undulating glittering pathway, a golden track charted on the surface of the ocean which our ship followed unswervingly until the sun dipped below the edge of the horizon, and the pathway ran ahead of us faster than we could steam and slipped over the edge of the skyline – as if the sun had been a golden ball and had wound up its thread of gold too quickly for us to follow.'

Wanting to find our more about the man, I contacted his daughter Dinah, who told me a little more about her father and what it was like growing up with such a well-respected (and by now famous) *Titanic* survivor:

'I was born in 1913 when the *Titanic* was still pretty fresh in people's minds. By the time I was old enough to understand what my father had been through the subject was rarely spoken of. The point is that he was so moved by the *Titanic* disaster, more I think that people realised. He kept an enormous scrapbook about it which I found fascinating. I would pore over it in my spare hours trying to imagine what it had been like for him, because it was something he didn't like to talk about a great deal.

I remember he once told me why it made him feel the way it did. He recalled the pitiful screams of the people in the water after the ship went down – and then the terrible silence. That left a marked impression on him which lasted his whole life. He didn't show it in any obvious way and he kept his innermost thoughts to himself. He never had the desire to go on another ship again. His distaste of the sea in general manifested itself most clearly when one year the family went for a beach holiday. He simply turned his deckchair around so that he had his back to the ocean. Nothing would induce him to even look at his family splashing about in the water. A stranger would have thought that eccentric, but of course we knew he had once seen many hundreds of people helpless and afraid, fighting for their lives that night all those years ago.

All kinds of people wanted to talk to him about the *Titanic* and he was consulted regularly for his opinion on various aspects of the disaster. In that way, he simply couldn't leave it behind. In the 1950s he was asked to assist in the making of the film *A Night to Remember*. He didn't really want to do it but he felt that if he could be of some use in dispelling the myths about it he would help in any way he could. My sister Laurien went with him to the studios where a section of the *Titanic* had been reproduced. Heaven knows why, but one day during filming he took it upon himself to become an extra in the film and got himself dressed in appropriate 1912-style clothes and inveigled himself into the crowds 'on deck'. However, just as the camera was about to roll he was spotted and respectfully asked to leave. Imagine the irony of that! It was the second time he found himself leaving the *Titanic* before it sank!

After the filming was over I accompanied my father to the premiere in London. He enjoyed the film for its accuracy and style. I sometimes wonder what on earth he would make of the never-ending interest in the *Titanic* today. I think he would be amazed that his book was still so popular. I myself recently re-read it after a space of many years and found it just as gripping as the first time. I enjoyed the recent film too [James Cameron's *Titanic*] as I'm sure my father would have done.

Nonetheless, it is rather incredible to think people are so very taken with the subject, isn't it?

When I was a girl, I would sometimes have friends over for tea. They were amazed that my father would allow me to chatter and ask questions at the meal table. In those days it was very much a case of children being 'seen and not heard'. But that was my father – so tolerant and patient and so interested in what we had to say, all our little discoveries. He adored us and positively encouraged us to think independently and use our minds. His great passion was golf and he became rather good at it. In fact, he taught us all to play. He was a born teacher and taught more or less up until the end of his life. It was his vocation.

After reaching New York on board the *Carpathia* my father found a gold sovereign in his pocket that he'd put there at some point before the *Titanic* sank. It has been passed down in the family and eventually came to me. I had it linked on to a necklace some time ago. When I wear it now I think of that kind and gentle man who was not only my father but who so narrowly escaped with his life on that night in 1912.'

LUSITANIA
(1915)

19 January 2002

A visit to see Audrey Pearl this afternoon to talk about how she survived the sinking of the *Lusitania* on 7 May 1915. A charming hostess who was most accommodating even though I must have worn her out with my questions.

No collection about disasters at sea in the 21st century could be complete without the *Lusitania* in it. Until I made contact with Audrey Pearl last year I honestly thought the last of the survivors had passed away. There is a mountain of first-hand accounts by *Lusitania* survivors long dead, but I always prefer human contact above archival research because it brings the experience 'alive' for me. Which brings me back to the present. After a lengthy correspondence, I was invited for tea today and I was there like a shot. As far as I know she is the last survivor and I was so very keen to hear her story first-hand because as a baby Audrey Pearl was saved from the *Lusitania* when it sank beneath her. As a woman she learned that it was her mission to help others in peril on the sea.

Audrey Pearl's parents had had some pretty interesting adventures before boarding the *Lusitania* on its final voyage in May 1915. Three years earlier they had been booked on the *Titanic*. As they were both Americans with family ties in England, it was quite routine for them to make frequent journeys across the Atlantic. However, something came up that made them change their plans, so the *Titanic* sailed into history without them. Later, on a research project in Belgium, Major Surgeon Pearl was arrested for being a spy because of his 'foreign' accent and thrown into Lubeck Prison. Horrified, Mrs Pearl jumped on the next available ship in order to clear up the error. She found herself under interrogation for 4 hours and it took some very persuasive arguments on her part before her husband was released. 'Quite an experience, I shouldn't wonder,' commented Audrey Pearl dryly.

Being a medical man with a strict sense of duty, Major Surgeon Pearl was anxious to tend to the war-wounded in Europe. Both parents were also inclined to have their children educated in England at a later date, so they made plans to travel to the UK. They would not be slumming it, however. Mr and Mrs Warren Pearl, their four children and two nannies would be travelling in the opulent first class.

What the Pearl family probably did not know was that the *Lusitania* was in fact by now also officially classed as an armed merchant cruiser. On Government orders the ship had been fitted out with guns and was carrying a supply of ammunition intended for Allied use. As such she was deemed a legitimate target for enemy submarines. The German Imperial Embassy politely placed a tidy little advert alongside promotional material for Cunard departures warning people of the danger. However, for this trip 290 first class passengers, 600 second, 367 third and 702 members of the crew were prepared to take the risk. Since America was a neutral country at that time, it was widely assumed that any ship carrying American citizens would be excluded from attack. Sadly, the assumption was wrong.

The *Lusitania* was torpedoed and sunk by German submarine U-20 just off Old Head of Kinsale on 7 May 1915. In less than 20 minutes she was at the bottom of the Irish Sea. The overall death toll came to 1,195 people. Shockingly, only 27.1% of the children on board survived the ordeal. Audrey Pearl was a very lucky girl indeed.

AUDREY PEARL

❝ My mother was from New York and my father was a native Bostonian. I was born in New York and was to become one of seven children eventually. There was my eldest brother Stuart, my two elder sisters Susan and Amy, then me. My mother was pregnant with my brother Warren during the voyage on the *Lusitania* and after the disaster she had a boy and a girl.

Most of what I know about that time on the *Lusitania* comes from Alice Lines, my devoted nurse, as I was only three months old at the time. She was a wonderfully spirited woman. She came over to America and lied about her age when she got the position with our family. I suppose she was only about fifteen or something like that. If it wasn't for her I simply wouldn't be alive today. Stuart and I were in Alice's care while Amy and Susan had their own nanny to look after them.

On the day in question it was bright and sunny, so my parents had decided to take coffee in the Veranda Cafe (that in itself was unusual because my mother usually professed to disliking coffee). Suddenly there was a terrific bang and my father said straight away, 'We've been hit by a torpedo.' I suppose being a military man he knew what he was talking about. This was followed by a second thunderous explosion.

Meanwhile, Stuart and I were down in our cabin with Alice. It was pretty obvious that something was terribly wrong with the ship so Alice grabbed me and wrapped me in a shawl around her neck – rather like a sling I suppose – and took Stuart by the hand – he was only five – and struggled up to the boat deck.

There were scenes of terrible confusion. Many of the crew were inexperienced and the launching of the lifeboats was mismanaged. Nobody knew where their lifeboat station was, so people panicked. A sailor grabbed Stuart and dropped him into a lifeboat but wouldn't let Alice in as it was too full already. She was desperate. So when she saw the boat being lowered she made a jump for it. But she had misjudged her timing and fell between the boat and the ship into the sea. So many people died that day from exposure that it's a miracle that either of us survived. Alice had just missed some wreckage that was bobbing about in the water and had she hit it we would surely both have died.

It so happened that Alice's hair was hanging loose that day (she hadn't had time to pin it up in the rush) and strangely enough it saved both our lives. As she struggled to keep hold of me with one hand and reach for the surface with the other, her hair streamed out like a fan. Suddenly a man grabbed it from above and pulled her to the surface. Can you imagine how painful that must have been? Anyway, she and I were dragged into the same boat that minutes earlier she had missed, and there was Stuart happily sitting on a woman's lap without a care in the world. I, on the other hand, burst into tears.

The next thing that happened is even more remarkable. A Frenchman noticed Alice and offered to look after her now that she was 'all alone in the world'. Years later, Alice told me that it must have been the first time someone had ever been proposed to during the sinking of a ship! Our lifeboat made its way back to the coast, which was about eight or ten miles away, and we didn't arrive until nine o'clock at night. Fortunately the weather was pretty good and that helped. Someone had organised a list of survivors and my parents were there waiting when we turned up. Stuart rushed into my mother's arms and said, 'Mummy, you've got a black eye!', which she did as both she and my father had had a terrible time of it. Amy and Susan were not so lucky. They were both trapped inside the ship and never made it.

Later, my parents were taken to Government House in Ireland and waited there for three months hoping that their daughters' bodies would be found, but they never were. You see, all the electricity failed pretty soon after the torpedo hit, so many people were left in complete darkness inside. I expect the nurse had the children with her and was trying to make her way up to the deck but got lost in the labyrinth of corridors. It must have been a nightmarish experience.

My mother had such strong religious faith. Naturally she was devastated by the loss of Amy and Susan, but she theorised that one day they would be reunited in heaven and this belief helped her cope with the trauma. She knew they had gone to a better place. After the disaster she told us to never complain or grumble about anything as we had been spared.

The disaster changed everything for a while. We travelled on to England and stayed in Hampshire for a few months until my parents decided to continue with their original plan by moving us all to Brussels. Stuart was left behind because he had started boarding school.

Strangely enough, it didn't put any of us off travelling by ship. Apart from it being the only way to get across the Atlantic in those days, and therefore a necessity, we none of us were deterred by the experience. Cunard gave us all a perpetual 25% discount on their ships in light of the disaster, so we took full advantage of that. My mother always said that the *Lusitania* tragedy was the Germans' doing, *not* the sea's, and I rather agree with her.

I went on many transatlantic liners and you must remember that between the wars it was a halcyon time for that type of travel. I remember the *Normandie* particularly well as being a splendid vision of art deco, as was the *Ile de France*. They were simply stunning. I adored the *Queen Mary* of course, and we also went on a number of White Star ships like the *Majestic* and *Georgic*. I even went on the *Mauretania*, and if anything was going to put me off you'd think it would have been that, but it didn't. You just had to pull yourself together and get on with it.

If anyone found out that you had been on the *Lusitania* they were fascinated and would want to talk to you about it for hours. I even remember on one ship bumping into a deck steward who had been on the *Lusitania* too. We had quite an interesting chat!

My mother and I often went to visit a survivor called Rita Jolivet, who was an actress. Believe it or not she made two films about the disaster. She lived in Monte Carlo at the time and was retired by then. She was utterly charming. Aside from that it was a subject taken for granted in the family and rarely talked about.

I feel that the *Lusitania* has been somewhat overshadowed by the *Titanic*, yet it was just as bad. I have only been interviewed once before about my experiences, for the TV, and that was with Alice and mother back in the 'sixties. I certainly haven't been to any reunions or anything like that. I wouldn't dream of writing about my experiences, as who would want to read it? There's nothing I can add to all the other books written about the disaster. I suppose it was just another ship lost during the Great War and when so many people were dying every day people didn't dwell on it and I've never given it a great deal of thought until recently.

The family always kept in touch regularly with Alice Lines until her death two years ago at the age of a hundred. She had married twice and had celebrated two silver weddings. She lived down in Bexhill-on-Sea and we often used to see her. My brother Stuart settled in England and became a lawyer. He died many years ago from emphysema. My father passed away in 1954 and my mother outlived him for exactly ten years. At the end of her life she said she knew more people on the 'other side' waiting for her than in this world. Dying didn't appear to worry her too much because her faith was so very strong. The son my mother was carrying during the sinking is still alive. We always called him 'Perky' because he was so upbeat all the time – full of life – and he *adored* the sea!

I don't agree with people salvaging things from the wreck at all. My two sisters are there somewhere, not to mention all the other poor souls that went down with her. It doesn't seem right to me. I think it should be treated as a war grave and left in peace. Even though my sisters' bodies were never found, we had two graves made for them some time ago. There is, I believe, a fine memorial to the victims in Queenstown and a museum, which I should like to see one day.

My mother always believed passionately that if you had the means you should give something back to society, and she was a wonderful patroness of various charities. Eventually she won the CBE for her involvement with good works. I have been raising money for two years now to have a lifeboat launched for the RNLI, which will be named the *Amy Lea* – in honour of my mother. Before he died Stuart had also been involved, as he felt strongly about helping in some way. So far it's going very well and I'm thrilled about it. I only wish Stuart were still here to see it come to fruition.

I had a lucky escape early in life and know what it is to come close to death. This is my way of saying thank you.

22 March 2002

An interesting addition to the story Audrey Pearl related to me is this account by her father Major Warren Pearl, which is an official statement he gave at the time. It is interesting because of how it differs from Alice Lines's recollections and also for the stance Major Pearl takes on the affair – no recriminations at all, no lambasting of the Cunard Line, and not a hint that he must have been devastated by the loss of his two little girls – which he so clearly was, according to his daughter. A sense of Edwardian stoicism pervades the whole account:

MAJOR WARREN PEARL

66 At about 2.00pm I went below to E deck, the portholes of which were about 16 feet above the waterline. I was in a room on E deck, port side. 15 minutes later I heard an explosion on the opposite side of the ship. My wife and nurse had been drilled as to what to do in an emergency. Flames, smoke and broken glass from port holes blew into our stateroom. My wife was on deck at the time. She saw the torpedo coming from the starboard side, which hit the ship about eight seconds later. My wife went below and there was no panic. We met and sent the nurse and children on the deck and followed them to the boat deck. We put on life belts which later proved their excellence by their great sustaining power. The boat deck was crowded but there was no panic or shrieking. In coming on deck the ship's wake showed she had made a swing of nearly a semicircle to port. In the crowd the nurse, stewardess and the three children got separated from my wife. One of the nurses and one of our children were standing by a boat, which was swung out and ready for launching.

The ship was listing to starboard but soon righted herself. I was searching the boat deck for the missing nurse and children. I found two boats lowered on the starboard side, a third suspended perpendicularly in mid-air. There were women and children being put in a fourth preparatory to lowering. There was no confusion so far. I went back to my wife when word came to 'Lower the boats – Everything's all right – Aid Coming'. I made a second tour of the deck to find the children. Unable to find them I went back to see if they were with my wife but they were not with her. My wife asked me to try again to find them. The ship was on a fairly even keel. Just now a boat filled with people hanging from davits crashed inward, falling on people on the deck. The ship suddenly made a forward plunge to starboard, water rushing in over the forecastle-head and decks. The missing children were still not found. I took two planks for my wife and nurse and child when the sea came rushing aft, throwing everyone on deck into the sea as the ship plunged beneath. I was pulled down five or six times by suction and eddies. In coming to the surface I got one plank. Later I swam to a floating box with five or six others clinging to it. This overturning, I got hold of a deckchair and later swam with it to a floating tin can. I clung to this for about three hours. Three passing boats being full could not take me up. After about three hours in the water I was picked up by men in a collapsible boat half full of water which was being bailed out. Discipline in this boat was excellent. We picked up about 35 people in all and several women.

About one hour later we were taken off by a steam trawler which went about rescuing many others, finally landing us at Queenstown about eight hours after the sinking of the ship. My wife had been swept into the sea by the same wave as myself. She was pulled onto the bottom of the overturned boat on which were about fifty people, disciplining those who were over-excited. After about two and a half hours on this boat she was hoisted on board a tramp steamer, where she received every possible kindness and care...

Titanic threads...
Nancy Mitford

A letter today from the Duchess of Devonshire. I had so enjoyed my visit to Chatsworth House in Derbyshire that I wrote and told her. I must say that, with all the things she has to do to keep that place going, I was surprised to receive such a long, handwritten reply.

As Deborah Mitford before her marriage she came from one of those large Edwardian aristocratic families that by today's standards seem positively a world apart. However, after visiting Chatsworth it's clear that the warm and homely feeling about the place is very much down to the present Duke and Duchess. It's also fun. Getting out of the car next to the house I was met by a nonchalant chicken, then another and another. They didn't seem to take much notice of me or the other visitors and seemed skilfully adept at dodging traffic.

Deborah's sister Nancy is by far one of my favourite writers – a sort of Jazz Age Jane Austen. I re-read *Love in a Cold Climate* at least once every year. Her sparkling prose is a continual joy to me – and how I envy her style! Inspired to find out more about the author, I've started reading Selena Hastings's biography. It wasn't long before the *Titanic* made an appearance – and a fittingly singular one at that. In 1913 Nancy was being looked after by her indomitable Nanny while her parents ('Farve' and 'Muve' – Lord and Lady Redesdale) were prospecting gold in Canada:

'Nancy wrote dutifully to her parents, "Dear Muve and Farve, is the shack nice?" while nursing the secret hope that they, like the ill-fated passengers of the *Titanic*, on which the Redesdales originally had booked passages and which had gone down the year before, would be lost at sea, thus leaving the reins of the household in her small but capable hands, an unparalleled opportunity to boss the others. Every morning she scanned Nanny's *Daily News* for a report of the wreck. Toiling up Victoria Road after Nanny and the pram holding Pam and Diana [Nancy's younger sisters], she would ask, "How big is the *Titanic*?" "As big as from here to Kensy High Street," Nanny would reply, leaving in the child's mind an impression that would remain for life of the *Titanic* as Victoria Road, houses, trees and all, steaming through the icebergs.'

RAWALPINDI
(1939)

2 February 2002

To Kent to meet Roy Leadbetter. He doesn't seem fazed by the memory of how he just managed to escape with his life when the *Rawalpindi* sank on 23 November 1939. Is it that the passing years have dampened the nerve-jangling memories of it, or is it more simple than that? Did people just 'get on with it' and put these experiences behind them? The more I encounter people like him the more I admire them for their outright determination not to let things like wars and sinking ships ruin their lives. I admire their guts too.

Like many young men Roy Leadbetter craved adventure. He knew it wasn't going to come to him in his position as a commis waiter in a London hotel, so when his mate suggested he tried stewarding on the liners he jumped at the chance. Yearning for exotic far-off lands, he joined the P&O company in 1939 together with his younger brother Jack. A few days after war was declared, they were both signed on to the *Rawalpindi*, a modest-sized ship that undertook the China-Bombay run. Kitted out in their tropical white uniforms, they looked forward to crystal blue seas and balmy weather. Instead they found themselves shivering on patrol in the foggy, grey Scapa Flow.

The *Rawalpindi* had been requisitioned by the British Admiralty as an armed merchant cruiser and was placed under the command of Captain E. C. Kennedy – father of the TV presenter, journalist and writer Ludovic Kennedy. With its second funnel removed, the luxury fittings stripped away and her hull repainted an austere battleship grey, the *Rawalpindi* presented quite a different picture of cruise life from the one the brothers had expected.

In addition to their regular duties as saloon stewards, the Leadbetters also had to keep a constant supply of ammunition for the gunner. Sometimes to while away the hours they would use passing icebergs for target practice. But the war was never very far away and both men were horrified to witness the sinking of the *Royal Oak* and *Iron Duke* with great loss of life.

The *Rawalpindi* was to last only two months of the war. On 23 November she encountered the German battle-cruisers *Scharnhorst* and *Gneisenau*, which opened fire on her. With her midships ablaze and her bridge and wireless room destroyed, the crippled ship foundered within three hours. Among the casualties were Captain Kennedy and 275 crew.

Of the 37 survivors who evacuated the ship before she sank, 26 were picked up by the German cruisers and taken prisoner of war. The remaining 11 were more successful. Having managed to launch a lifeboat during a lull in the action, they were rescued by another converted P&O liner, the *Chitral*.

Roy Leadbetter had wanted adventure and on the *Rawalpindi* he soon found it. However, as he told me today, 53 years after the event, it came at a high price.

ROY LEADBETTER

❝ By the time I boarded the *Rawalpindi* at the age of twenty-two as an officer's steward I was the main breadwinner in my family. I was the eldest of six children and by the early 'thirties my father upped and left leaving my mother to bring us all up single-handed. Exactly half of my wages were sent off to my mother in Staffordshire every month because the youngest two were still at school.

It was no holiday on the *Rawalpindi*. The days were long and we worked hard for our wages. I would get up at six and spend the next few hours cleaning the companionways and making cups of tea for the night watch officers. At half past seven it was time to serve the officers their breakfast and wait on table. Captain Kennedy was a real gent and very popular on the ship. Every night he would get us all together in the smoking room and talk about the progress of the war. He was well-informed and popular with the crew. The only real rest I got was during the lull between lunch and dinner. I would be sound asleep by ten o'clock, only the sirens would invariably go and off you would go to your battle station. That was the thing about war, you didn't get a lot of sleep.

Half way into our third patrol at 3pm, November 23rd 1939, the alarm bells sounded and I made my way up to the boat deck. Being so far north it was almost dark and *freezing* cold. In the poor light it was just possible to see two grey shapes approximately five miles away. It was quiet and at first we thought it was one of our own ships mistaking us for the enemy. Captain Kennedy and a midshipman came by and we were informed that there was a German ship near us and we were going to lay in smoke screen in order to shield ourselves and make a get-away. There was already thick black smoke coming from the funnel but the smoke floats designed for the job of screening us failed to work.

When I had first gone to sea I had bought myself a telescope and I happened to have it on the *Rawalpindi*. An officer came up to me and asked if he could borrow it so that he could get a better view of the enemy. No sooner had he done so than there was a terrific explosion and he was nearly thrown over into the water. He pulled himself together and crawled over to me saying, 'Lucky escape!' and I replied, 'Never mind that, what about my telescope!' The blast had practically bent it double, and the poor fellow's eye socket had been almost gouged out. I didn't care about him – it was the state of my telescope that bothered me!

After a short while the German ships separated so that there was one on each side of us. Their aim was good – or at least one of them was. Our guns opened up in retaliation and we hit one of the ships several times, causing a number of casualties. I had gone to the ammunition hoist to get some star shells, but when I returned my gun and fellow gun crew had all been blown into the water.

I knew it was getting pretty serious now so I went in search of my brother whose gun was on the fore well deck. However, when I arrived I found his gun was lying on its side with the remains of the bridge on it – and absolutely no signs of life to be seen. It was an odd feeling – standing there amongst the wreckage feeling completely alone. The only sound was the whistle of the shells and the muffled explosions coming from somewhere deep inside the ship. The sky was lit up by the inferno on the upper decks, making it almost as light as day, and while it was freezing cold outside, the heat from the fires made it unbearably hot. It was all a little unreal. I was starting to get frantic because I knew I had to find Jack. He was only nineteen and just a kid really. Eventually I stumbled on both him and a friend holed up in a paint locker in the forecastle. I rushed them on to the boat deck to see if any lifeboats were left but they all appeared to be damaged or on fire. The Germans at this stage were still firing, but at irregular intervals as they were giving the smaller guns an opportunity for fire practice. The *Rawalpindi* was listing a bit and badly damaged. Before the trip her hold had been loaded with empty oil drums which would act as giant floats to keep her up, and I presume it was these that kept her going for so long.

Somehow I managed to find two lifejackets. I put one on and the other I took to Jack. His mate pleaded with me to get him one too so I went off in search of another. When I got back they were both gone. I never saw either of them again.

By now it was getting extremely dangerous on the open deck and fire had broken out everywhere. In panic I made for a rope ladder which was hanging over the side of the ship. It seemed a safer bet there as the other side was being shelled and battered something terrible. Trouble was, the ship was still making headway even though no one was alive on the bridge to steer her and I knew that if I didn't jump clear enough away from her I would have been sucked under and drowned. As I was hanging on wondering what to do, a lad lunged past me screaming, his back completely ablaze, and dived into the sea. I shall never forget that scream. It was like nothing I'd ever heard before. Suddenly, a few feet away, there was a shower of sparks where an armour-piercing shell went through the hull. Time to go, I thought, but not this way. So I changed my mind about jumping and clambered back on to the deck.

About the only place not enveloped by fire was the stern, so those few of us that were left made our way there. Unfortunately, we realised pretty soon that we were in fact sitting on the depth charges in their racks. Not the best place to be on a burning ship! I knew that one lifeboat had made it off some time before, but now the *Rawalpindi* was in its death throes and I wondered if I would get off alive. I wasn't scared, just intent on saving myself. There was always the hope that Jack had made it and I couldn't give up yet. As the list grew more pronounced a lifeboat fell over the side into the sea. By the time I saw it it was about 100 yards away so I decided it was my last chance and into the sea I dropped.

I didn't notice how cold the water was – I guess my mind was so focused on survival. I was a non-swimmer but with my lifebelt on I somehow managed to reach the lifeboat before anyone else. However, I simply couldn't pull myself over the side of the boat with this bulky thing around me so very carefully I removed it, flung it into the boat and climbed in. I honestly don't know how I had the strength to do it. I was panic-stricken, breathless and shivering like mad. The boat was half full of water, which didn't help, and the weather was nasty, making the likelihood of the boat capsizing pretty real. Had the boat sunk I would surely have drowned because I didn't have the strength to do another thing.

Eventually, ten of the crew made it to the boat. There would have been more but we were unable to row the boat as all the oars, except the steering oar, had been swept away when the lifeboat had fallen overboard.

We gradually drifted away and watched as the *Rawalpindi* blew up and finally sank. One of the German ships saw us and stopped while we drifted towards it. The crew shouted any number of obscenities down to us in perfectly good English and then added, 'Sorry we cannot stop, one of your ships is near. Good night and good luck.' And off they went into the night, nearly drowning us in their wash. Now we were completely alone with no guarantee of rescue and very little in the way of supplies.

By now it was about 6pm and completely dark. The sea was rough and getting worse. Gradually we got some of the water out of the lifeboat and found the plug hole and screwed it shut. We used bits of rag to plug up the holes in the sides of the boat caused by the enemy fire earlier on. The buoyancy tanks that had holes in them were put on the seats to break the strong wind. In this fashion we passed a night, with an occasional spell at bailing out. During the night it snowed, but that saved us from getting thirsty as we were able to lick the snowflakes off our clothes. I was wearing a long Navy-issue jumper, which kept my upper body protected from the biting wind and the worst of the cold. The only food in the lifeboat lockers was sweetened condensed milk tins and ships biscuits. The milk was hard, so we took it in turns to urinate on the tins to soften it up. The biscuits had to be chewed by those with good teeth and passed to the men who could not chew as they were impossibly hard little things. By daylight we were past caring, all frozen and sleepy, feet and hands badly swollen, after being in the freezing water for so long.

At about 2pm we sighted a ship but it took over an hour before we were seen. The steering oar with an oil skin tied to it was all we had to attract their attention and it was getting dark, which made visibility a problem. Luckily a look-out spotted us and we were saved. The ship was the *Chitral*, another P&O liner converted to an armed cruiser just like the *Rawalpindi*. They threw us a rope down and hauled us up. I was taken into the kitchen where it was warm and had my limbs rubbed to get the circulation going. From my toes to my knees my skin had blistered badly. My penis had also retracted up into my groin due to the cold (fortunately it came out again once I warmed up!). I recognised a few mates in the crew and that made me feel more at home.

Another lad was picked up from an overturned lifeboat just drifting by. He was practically frozen on to the keel of the boat and they had to literally prize him off. Originally there had been other lads clinging to it but during the night they had all died of exposure. As for the first lifeboat to get away, they were not so lucky. There had been about twenty crew on it and they were picked up by one of the German ships and taken prisoner of war.

A week later we landed in Glasgow. From there we were sent to London for the official enquiry and then sent home with a rail warrant and £5. Meanwhile, my mother had received two telegrams – one telling her that I was alive and the other informing her of Jack's death. For a while I hoped that he had been taken prisoner in the other boat, but he went down with the ship. My mother applied for a pension to support her and the family now that Jack was dead, and this was immediately terminated when I went back to work after two weeks. So after fourteen days I was once again the breadwinner. In those days your pay stopped the minute the voyage ended, even if the ship didn't make it back to port. I was employed by the Royal Navy as an auxiliary on the *Rawalpindi* and they didn't give me a bean. The minute the ship sank I was unemployed.

It didn't stop me from going to sea though. During and after the war I served on many of the finest ships in the world, including the *Queen Mary* and *Queen Elizabeth*. I've waited on the powerful and the rich and I've loved every minute of it. How many people can say they've seen Churchill roaring drunk or been told blue jokes by Lord Mountbatten? Some of my happiest times have been spent at sea and the *Rawalpindi* wasn't ever going to put me off. I got to see the world just as I'd planned at a time when travelling by ship was really *something*.

Titanic threads...
Joanna Spreckley

A few months after I started this diary, L. and I motored down to the New Forest to have tea with Joanna Spreckley – a 99-year-old lady who served as a VAD [Voluntary Aid Detachment] in the First World War. I've long been interested in talking to people who went through the Edwardian period and the cataclysmic events of 1914-18. Joanna Spreckley came from a wealthy family and would have enjoyed the pleasures of house parties, debutante balls and the like had the war not intervened. She was born to a life a privilege, but came to know hardship and hunger during her time as a volunteer nurse.

I told her about my meeting with Millvina Dean. In a flash she became quite animated and told me all about hearing of the *Titanic* disaster as the news filtered into London:

'One year we were in No 9 Elvaston Place, Kensington, and our horses were sent up from Stroud so that we could ride in the Park. It was during that time that the *Titanic* was sunk, and there being no radio in those days the streets were full of newsboys calling out the news, 'SINKING OF THE TITANIC!' And I remember rushing into the house calling out to my parents that I had heard the newsboy say that the *Titanic* had sunk. No one would believe it. 'Don't be so ridiculous!' said my mother. 'The *Titanic* is unsinkable.'

It seems like everyone I meet has something to say about the *Titanic*. However, it always gives me a thrill to hear little stories like Joanna's because, *unlike* most people, she was actually *there* as history was being made.

CITY OF NAGPUR
(1941)

23 February 2002

An afternoon well spent. Elizabeth Dunn is jolly good company and there is a distinct lack of artifice in her conversation. She just tells it how it is and lets you make up your mind about it.

The entire course of Elizabeth Dunn's life changed after the sinking of the *City of Nagpur*. Had history taken a different path she may well have lived out the rest of her days as a South African housewife. As it turned out, fate had other plans for her.

Sixty years on there is still something of the free spirit in Elizabeth Dunn. With her wry sense of humour and total lack of sentimentality, she related the last voyage of the *City of Nagpur* to me, and its demise. The young Elizabeth certainly evinced a fearless streak in her character when she decided to make the hazardous wartime crossing from Glasgow to Freetown to join her husband who was on training duty there with the RAF. But as she told me, 'You do lots of crazy things when you're young.'

On 29 April 1941, about 700 miles west of Fastnet, the *City of Nagpur* was torpedoed and sunk by German submarine U-75. Mercifully, the majority of passengers and crew were saved, due in no small measure to the generosity of Kapitanleutnant Ringelmann, who gave them extra time to evacuate the ship.

The Ellerman Line ship *City of Nagpur* had a relatively brief career – 21 years in all. She had been built for the Glasgow-Bombay run and later reverted to the London-Africa service. Each summer the ship was made available for the lucrative cruise trade. At the outbreak of the Second World War she took up military duties and served in a combined capacity as troop transport and civilian carrier. Elizabeth Dunn remembers the public lounges and bars, which still retained something of their pre-war glamour, but the 'big bonus' was the food, which was far tastier than the grim wartime rations back in England.

As Elizabeth Dunn watched mesmerised from her lifeboat as the *City of Nagpur* settled deeper and deeper into the dark water, she could have had no idea that it was more than her clothes and belongings that she had lost.

ELIZABETH DUNN

❝ When the war broke out in 1939 I was already married to a peacetime RAF officer who was straight away called up to go and train British pilots in South Africa. We had only been married for a very short time and were both incredibly young – too young really to know what we were getting into. I was able to get a passage on board the *City of Nagpur* in order to join him in Cape Town in April 1941.

I had been raised in a small village in Malvern and the war had brought enormous changes to us. The RAF had a station there and later on the American and Canadian lads arrived, which, of course, generated a huge amount of excitement. In fact, four of the girls from our village went back to America with their sweethearts after the war. The RAF officers were really like film stars to us – they were so dashing and handsome – and John (my husband to be) was by far the best. Every girl in the village wanted him and I thought, 'Well, why not me?' So we started walking out and eventually it led to marriage. My father, who was the local parson, conducted the marriage service and for a while everything was wonderful. Then we were separated and naturally I was obliged to follow him.

I didn't really want to go. In my heart of hearts there was part of me that just wanted to carry on as before. What happened later on was actually quite a God-send. I had never been out of England and South Africa seemed such a long way away, but I applied for a permit to go and join him and it was granted in April '41, so, after an emotional send-off, I left.

I was travelling alone. I picked up the ship in Gourock, Scotland. The *Nagpur* was a smallish ex-cruise ship. The officers who ran the ship were British, but all the crew, stewards and so forth were Indian Laskers who were wearing their own dress, which looked extremely exotic to me. It was fascinating to see them in the evening serving dinner in all their finery. I believe the ship was originally banded by class, but at this time everyone was simply allocated a cabin and the class thing was disbanded. The other passengers were largely made up of women and children, some married couples and quite a few service personnel who were to be dropped off on the way at Freetown and some in Aden. But by far the biggest proportion of passengers were the women.

The ship had not been altered inside for war service. I recall there being charming lounges and smoking rooms and so on. My cabin – which I was lucky enough not to have to share – was pretty basic: no running water, for instance, and if you wanted a bath you rang for a Lascar who would position an old-fashioned hip bath in the room and fill it with water for you by hand. But it was very comfortable and of course the food was a delight – infinitely better than anything we had back home. That was a big bonus.

I later learned that the *Nagpur* was equipped with guns, because when we were attacked the crew fired them. However, I don't remember seeing them up until the night of the sinking. Early in the trip we were all issued with a small card, which told us where our lifeboat station was, and there was a drill. The problem was that although we practised the drill, the boats were never actually lowered to test them out, and that is where the trouble occurred later on when they were needed for real.

Naturally there was no entertainment provided on the ship as there would have been in peacetime, but everyone was terribly friendly. Between meals we would walk around the decks or chat in one of the lounges and I suppose, being young, we none of us ever considered the danger. I made friends with two chaps from the outset – one of them an officer on the ship who was on his way to Aden – and I never felt lonely. People were like that during the war, you see. Complete strangers would help you. You just never knew what was around the corner, so you put yourself out to be kind or friendly. It was very much like that on the ship. We all got along terribly well. Everyone was very optimistic during the voyage, no fear or anything like that.

The weather hadn't been bad at all on the trip. It was Spring and we were able to walk on the promenade decks quite freely during the day so we were lucky in that respect. There were no other ships with us, no convoy. We were completely alone. After a couple of days we came into contact with another ship, but after a while it received a radio message to pick up survivors from a shipwreck and it went off to help. We couldn't go because the *Nagpur* was full to capacity already. After that we were on our own again.

It was one o'clock in the morning when the first torpedo hit the ship. About fifteen of us were having a little after-dinner drink in the smoking room and the party was breaking up when it happened. I was actually being escorted back to my cabin by an officer and another chap and we were almost thrown off balance. There was a huge bang and a bit of commotion. The ship immediately appeared to take on a list, but then slowly righted herself. I never made it back to my room at all. My chaperones took me straight to the lifeboat station. There was no panic, but all the same people were flying about everywhere, half-dressed in most cases. Most people were asleep at the time, so they appeared bleary-eyed with bewildered, children in tow, and stumbled along as best they could. Many of them didn't even have time to get a coat, but I was lucky because I was already dressed in a wool dress and fur coat.

As we made our way to the lifeboat station I remember seeing various Laskers pulling blankets and green baize tablecloths out of lockers and bundling them into the boats. Lots of activity. The trouble was that as soon as the boats were lowered they jumped in first! I suppose they were terrified but it did cause a few raised eyebrows at the time. My two companions left me at the boat and then went off to their own stations and I didn't see them again until we got back to Scotland. I'd say the average age on that ship was twenty-five, and being as young as we were we just didn't consider the possibility of danger, *real* danger. You feel invincible at that age. Initially a few couples were separated, as were some of the mothers and children, and they were anxious about their loved ones but there was no hysteria or anything like that. There was nobody shouting 'WOMEN AND CHILDREN FIRST!' like on the *Titanic*. It was quite orderly.

It was only when the crew started to let the lifeboats out that they realised there was something wrong. The boats came down in sharp jerks instead of on an even keel and it was very dangerous. They clearly hadn't been tested for ages and were not terribly seaworthy. We were all standing in a group waiting to get on, and just as I was about to climb in I heard a disembodied German voice floating across the sea hollering, 'As there are women and children on board I am going to give you twenty minutes for you to evacuate the ship before I put another torpedo in.' It was quite extraordinary! It was a moonlit night and about seventy yards away you could see the outline of this U-boat. In fact, the Germans gave us an awful lot longer than twenty minutes, which was just as well as we were all of us able to get off in time. In the end he lost patience as it was taking so long and he did start shelling the ship, but all things considered he was pretty fair. The majority of the casualties came when the first torpedo hit and they were the engine room lads who didn't have a chance.

After all the boats got clear of the ship they were roped together for safety, leaving room enough so as not to bang into each other. The swell was pretty high so you'd only ever get glimpses of the other boats and then they would disappear for a few seconds and then up they'd appear again. The biggest problem was that the boats took on water straight away. In fact, you could actually see through the joins in the planking because they had shrunk so much! So everybody started bailing like fury using anything they had – hats, shoes, cups, anything. After a few hours the wood expanded and the joints sealed themselves. This just left a dirty, smelly, puddle sloshing about in the bottom.

We watched the submarine circle the ship and saw it put another torpedo into the other side. Almost immediately it started to sink by the head. It seemed to only take a few minutes at most. There was the most terrible whooshing sound as it went – something I can't quite describe as I've never heard anything like it since. And then it was simply gone. It struck me then that practically every possession I had in the world was lost. All I had were the clothes I was wearing.

We were in the lifeboats for about twelve hours in all. The worst thing was having to go for a pee as it was quite embarrassing in such a cramped space. It didn't bother the men – they just went over the side – but us women just had to make do with a bucket. It was mortifying! Eventually someone found some mouldy old biscuits and some cans of water of indeterminate age and we had some of that. Everyone was pretty hopeful – particularly the service personnel – that we would be rescued. It never even entered my head to think that we wouldn't! For most of the night we were a pretty quiet bunch, not a lot of talking or chat. I suppose everyone was just wrapped up in their own thoughts, thinking of home. Then as dawn broke a Catalina aircraft came flying over us. All the women were told to duck down into the bottom of the boat (which most of us didn't appreciate since it was wet and smelly), but the men didn't know whether it was an Allied or enemy plane. Finally someone recognised it as one of ours and they started morsing it with a flashlight. As it circled us it flashed back the message 'WILL SEND...' and because it was turning we couldn't get the last bit but we guessed in was 'HELP'. Well, we were all a great deal happier then. But it was another eight hours before a ship appeared on the horizon. Again, we didn't know if it was friendly or not so for the second time I found myself laying down in the stinky pool at the bottom of the boat. Luckily it was HMS *Hurricane*, which had received the wireless message and had come to save us.

The ship drew as close as it could to us and threw down a rope ladder. We were all in real danger now because if a ship sits dead in the water it is an easy target for attack. However, there was simply no other way. I must say that climbing that ladder was the hardest thing I've ever done. Being flush against the side of he ship it was difficult to get your feet in far enough to get a solid foothold, and because your hands are numb with cold it is almost impossible to get a grip. It was like climbing a mountain and I've never been so glad to get to the top! One lady had a baby in arms and she just couldn't manage it so a sailor climbed down, tucked the baby into the inside pocket of his greatcoat as if it were a rabbit and carefully scaled the ladder to safety.

Once we were on board the crew treated us with the utmost care and kindness. Our clothes were laundered and I was given a pair of men's trousers and a shirt to wear. The first thing they gave us was a bar of Cadbury's chocolate, which was simply heaven! We all ate in sittings and were given crew quarters to sleep in. Again, I was lucky enough to have my own cabin so I never had to 'rough it' at all going out or coming back. We were going to be dropped off in Gibraltar but the officials said they couldn't cope with the numbers so it was decided to take us back to England. We got there in two days because the ship was going at full speed. I was so relieved! My parents had heard from the Government that the ship had sunk but didn't know if I was OK or not until I got home. When we arrived in Scotland we were put up in a hotel and then given a train voucher to get us to our various destinations. You can imagine my parents' surprise on seeing be back so soon.

I never did get to South Africa. Eventually John and I met other partners, and though we tried once more at a reconciliation when he came home for his first leave, it never worked. We divorced and I never saw him again. Had I got there in 1941 my whole life would have been completely different, but looking back it all worked out for the best. Getting married at nineteen was ridiculous – you're just not ready for that kind of commitment, let alone during a war.

A few years ago, after my second husband died, I went on a cruise that took in South Africa on the itinerary. The tour guide asked us if anyone had been there before. I replied that I should have been there fifty years ago.

After telling him about the *Nagpur* I put it out of my mind until we were on a coach trip later on. At one point he stopped the coach and said to me, 'I've got something to show you, it won't take a minute.' So, leaving all the other passengers on the coach he took me into a newly built housing estate. I couldn't imagine what he was going to do, but then he stopped and pointed to an arch across the road. It turned out to be the entrance to the RAF training centre where John had been all those years before and where I would have gone to live with him. Now all that remained was the entrance, as the centre had been razed to the ground for the housing estate, but it did give me a strange feeling all the same. I don't believe in fate or anything like that, but had the *City of Nagpur* made it to South Africa all those years ago I wouldn't be talking to you now. Makes you think doesn't it?

Titanic threads...
Ellen Mary Walker

In July 2000 L. and I paid a visit to Ellen Mary Walker in Worcester. We came home in a sombre mood. Ellen was one of the many hundreds of children left behind when the *Titanic* sank. Her eyes frequently filled with tears as she told us her story. In a way, she's a metaphorical 'orphan of the *Titanic*' because the disaster literally robbed her of a father and denied her the love, care and support of her mother. The *Titanic* seems to have left a black mark on her life that she has never been able to rub away, not even to this day. Time has certainly not softened the blow. The contrast between her view on it and Millvina Dean's is marked. For Millvina Dean the *Titanic* has led to a post-retirement afterlife full of positive experiences. For Ellen Mary Walker the mantle of the *Titanic* seems to fill her with shame and disgust – despair even.

'The only thing the *Titanic* has ever meant to me is sorrow. Quite simply, it has ruined most of my life. I can't think why people are so interested in it today. There's nothing particularly good about it is there?

I was born at 34 Waterworks Road in Worcester. It was my grandparents' house actually – which backed on to the River Severn. My grandfather was chief engineer on the locks. I was so happy there; my grandmother used to make me the most lovely clothes and I went to a private convent school. One of my earliest memories was sitting in the family's punt while my grandfather strapped me into a special harness, saying, "We'll make sure you don't drown." I didn't know what he meant. For many years I thought my grandparents were my mum and dad because I never knew about my real mother until I was about twelve. It was a dreadful shock.

My mother was called Kate Phillips. At the age of nineteen she was working in a confectioners in Malvern owned by a man called Henry Morley. By today's standards Morley was practically a millionaire and owned shops in Birmingham and Worcester. Well, mother was an attractive young thing, I suppose, and Morley fell in love with her. He decided to take her away with him to San Francisco and start a new

47

life there. My mother was thrilled, of course – you can't blame her for that. She didn't have much of her own and this was a wonderful opportunity. He promised to marry her and together they would have a very comfortable life. The only problem was that he was already married and had a twelve-year-old daughter.

They assumed false names – Mr and Mrs Marshall – in order to get away. Morley sold his shares in the business to his brother Arthur so that he could get enough cash together for a hasty departure. They booked the first available passage to America, which happened to be on the *Titanic*'s maiden voyage. Naturally, it was a risky thing to do. He was leaving his wife and child, and only his brother knew where he was going. If they had got caught there would have been no end of trouble. I suppose they were just madly in love and desperately wanted to be together. There was no other way. To make matters more complicated, my mother was pregnant with me too. So, you see, they just had to go.

They were booked on to the second class which must have been a revelation for my mother. I mean, she had never known such luxury and splendour before, I'm sure. They must have been easy to spot in a crowd because my mother was tiny – under five foot – and Morley was over six foot tall! I expect they would have gone first class under any other circumstances (Morley could certainly afford it), but this way they would be less noticeable. They wanted to keep a low profile.

Of course, when the ship hit the iceberg Morley got my mother out of bed and into a lifeboat as soon as he knew the situation. I think that was part of the tragedy – nobody realised how dangerous it all was until it was too late. Anyway, he put my mother into boat 13 and kissed her goodbye. He was still in his nightclothes and my mother was only wearing her nightgown and slippers. Later on a sailor wrapped his jumper round her because it was so cold. She never saw Morley again. I've no idea where he is buried. Perhaps he was picked up later and laid to rest in Halifax. Otherwise I suppose he is at the bottom of the Atlantic…

I always remember, as a child, seeing this black valise in my grandmother's cupboard, which my mother had apparently carried off the ship with her. I don't see how this is possible because I'm sure the last thing most people were thinking about was their luggage. However, I was always told it was from the *Titanic*. That name didn't mean much to me at the time so I hardly paid any attention. Many years after that my mother showed me this beautiful sapphire and diamond pendant that Morley had given to her on the trip. She absolutely treasured that.

When the survivors were picked up by the *Carpathia* and taken on to New York, my mother was looked after by the American Red Cross. The Titanic Relief Fund gave her $300 and some clothing, which was just as well because she had lost everything. She must have felt terrible because she had nowhere to go – no husband, no future. Eventually she was brought back to England on the *Adriatic*.

Being pregnant now was the worst thing that could have happened to her. Can you imagine the scandal? It just wasn't done in those days. If you were a single mother people thought you were mentally retarded or something. She must have been frantic. That's why she landed up at my grandparents' where I was later born.

It was shameful for the entire family, but at least my grandparents stuck by mum. Morley's wife had only got $75 from the Titanic Relief Fund and that must have added insult to injury – after all, she was his *real* wife with a daughter to support. I don't suppose she even knew he had been on the *Titanic* until it was all over. It was the end of the road for my mother, though. She couldn't take the shame, the whispers. For all the help her mum and dad gave her, she couldn't stay in Worcester. Life was bad enough, without having a baby to look after, so she left me with my grandparents and went to start again in London. She was living in Ealing working in Lillian Skinner's shoe shop. Sometimes she came to visit but at that time I didn't know who she was – only that she would sweep in, cuddle me tightly, make a fuss of me, then leave again. I didn't like it and dreaded her visits. It wasn't until much later that I found out the truth.

Morley's brother said he would give mum a pound a week to look after me, and basically she needed the money. So she took me away when I was about twelve and it was a *dreadful* experience. I shudder when I think of her first words to me: "You're no longer a lady *now*, madam!" She was full or scorn and bitterness towards me. She dressed me in coarse black stockings and boots straight away. Thankfully she married a wonderful man called Frederick Watson who ran his own window-cleaning business. He saved my life really. Something had changed in my mother's personality. For some reason she was ever so cruel to me. She would lock me in a cupboard with just a pot in there to use as a toilet – sometimes for days. She would beat my legs with a stick and never once did she have a kind word to say to me... Eventually, my stepfather had to get a court order against my mother in order to stop her abusing me. What a kind, wonderful man he was.

It was the *Titanic* that made my mother so abusive towards me, pure and simple. You see, she had lost everything, her gorgeous new clothes, jewels, and a wonderful life with a man who could give her everything. She went from nothing to something, back to nothing again, and it broke her. There was no hope of ever escaping. Morley had promised her the world.

We moved to Ramsgate where my stepfather opened a cafe. I used to help out serving and waiting on tables but my mother just gave up on life. She took to her bed, repeatedly attempted suicide and eventually became mentally deranged. She had her room two floors above the cafe and would bang on the floor when she wanted something. Well, this got on my nerves – especially when it was busy in the shop – and one day I stormed up there and said, "Why don't you just put your head under the covers and snuff it!" She looked at me in terror and said, "Don't look at me that way. That's how your father looked at me the night he said goodbye to me on the *Titanic*." That was the first real information I had about him. Up until then I hardly knew a thing.

Mother died in a mental hospital in Shenley, Hertfordshire, in 1958. I didn't know she was dead until about three months later – we had completely drifted apart. I was married by then and had a child of my own to look after. Her death was a blessing. In her lucid moments she had given a few interviews about the *Titanic*, but on the whole it was a subject she rarely mentioned. It was far too painful for her – all her dreams shattered. I was the living embodiment of her troubles and she couldn't stand that.

During the Second World War I worked for the London Underground because all the men were off fighting. I enjoyed that and for once I was happy. However, I did have a nasty encounter with a doodlebug when it hit my house. The blast catapulted me through the door face first. My left eye actually popped out of its socket! I had to go to hospital for a few weeks so that they could sort me out. Miraculously it didn't affect my eyesight. After the war I went into the Central Passport Office in London and worked my way up to a chief officer's position. I stayed there until I retired.

My greatest wish it to have my father's name put on my birth certificate. At the moment it's blank and it just breaks my heart. After all these years who is it going to hurt? The Morley descendants don't want anything to do with me and they won't agree to DNA testing to prove he's my father once and for all. I hadn't even seen a *picture* of him until about twenty years ago when a local paper ran a story about three men from Worcester who had died on the *Titanic*. One of them was my father and they printed his photograph. I cried and cried when I saw his face. It was the most wonderful thing in the world. People have told me that they think my parent's story is romantic. I think it's the saddest thing you've ever heard.'

LACONIA
(1942)

3 April 2002

I've been reading up about the Nuremberg trials that took place in the aftermath of the Second World War. These hearings were set up to establish the exact involvement of captured Nazi party members in war crimes. One high-ranking defendant was Grand Admiral Dönitz who, after the sinking of the Cunard liner *Laconia* in September 1942, had issued the 'Laconia Order'. This directive meant that German U-boats were officially forbidden from rescuing any Allied survivors at sea. In Nuremburg, Dönitz found himself having to justify his decision in the glare of the world's press. I wonder how he would have felt having to explain his actions to survivors like Audrey Tiller, with whom I spoke today? A far more daunting prospect, I would have thought.

I suppose it's unusual to us today to consider that during the last war German forces periodically made goodwill gestures to their captors, or at least those at their mercy. However, Elizabeth Dunn, together with the other passengers on board the *City of Nagpur*, had been shown clemency by commander Kapitanleutnant Ringelmann. But the sinking of the *Laconia* was to change all that – officially at least.

On 12 September 1942, while en route from Suez to Great Britain, the *Laconia* was sighted by U-156 and torpedoed. The ship had an unusual passenger list as it was transporting 1,800 Italian prisoners of war, who were in turn guarded by 160 Polish troops (themselves former Russian POWs). In addition, there were 268 civilian and military personnel, including 80 women and children.

Five hundred Italian prisoners were killed instantly, while the rest of the passengers and crew desperately attempted to evacuate the ship. Help arrived – though from an unexpected quarter. Two German submarines, U-506 and U-507, offered assistance and embarked 200 people. Ironically, an American Liberator from 343 Squadron, USAF, dropped three depth charges near the submarines, either ignoring or misreading their Red Cross flag. A staggering 1,649 lives were lost when the *Laconia* foundered, making it (by casualty) the sixth worst disaster of the Second World War.

Her Captain, Rudolph Sharp, who had survived the *Lancastria* disaster two years earlier, also perished.

German naval authorities made it clear that henceforth no U-boats were to endanger themselves by stopping for survivors. Grand Admiral Dönitz was acquitted of this charge, but subsequently spent 11 years and 6 months in prison for other war crimes.

AUDREY TILLER

❝ My father was in the Royal Air Force so I was brought up in various RAF camps. In 1938, while stationed at RAF Cranwell in Lincolnshire, he was posted the North West Frontier in India. I had rheumatic fever, and since the doctor pronounced me unfit to travel my mother rented a house in Gosport for the following three years. However, an RAF medical officer then passed me as fit, so in 1939 we set off on the TS *Somersetshire* from Southampton. I was thirteen years old. In those days you were just a child at that age – no teenage years of course – we didn't know what that meant.

The first doctor was proved right. I spent the whole voyage in the ship's hospital. We were put off when the ship reached Port Said, Egypt. I ended up in the military hospital at Ismailia. My father received a compassionate posting to Egypt and we were sent eventually to an RAF camp about 5 miles from Ismailia. When Italy joined the war we were in danger of bombing, so we were put on the *Empress of Canada* and sent in convoy to Durban in South Africa, ending up in a hotel at the Uvongo Beach – about 50 miles from Durban. We stayed there until the summer of 1942. I was now healthy and at school studying for exams. Then out of the blue my father arrived with the news that after two weeks' leave we were to join the *Laconia* on 29 August at Durban.

My first impressions of the *Laconia* were that it was decidedly not as good as the *Empress of Canada*. The crew were pleasant enough, but definitely not cheerful. Our cabins were four-berth, but husbands were fed at different times from the wives and children, which was certainly not good for morale! There were a lot of servicemen aboard from all three forces, but it was mostly made up of Army lads. In addition, there were 1,493 Italian prisoners who were guarded by the Polish Army. All in all it was quite a mixed bunch.

We had deck tennis and film showings on board to keep us amused, so despite everything it was not unpleasant on board. The Garden Lounge was very attractive. Here we would be served tea and relax on pretty cane furniture. The library was also housed there too, and since I enjoyed reading that was a treat. We ate in the second class dining room, which was lovely although nobody took a blind bit of notice about class restrictions at this time.

We called in at Cape Town for three days, then left for Freetown. On 12 September there was to be a dance on board, starting at 8pm. I wasn't allowed to go, *much* to my consternation. My father simply said two words: 'Too young!' I was a bit miffed by this, as my friend Josie – who was the same age as me – had been given permission to go. Since I'd been allowed to attend the dances at the hotel, I went off to bed in a teenage huff, bemoaning my fate. It was the end of the world!

My parents left the cabin to go up to the deck where the dance was being held and I started to read. At about seven minutes past eight there was an almighty explosion from somewhere far below. The ship appeared to almost spin around, listing heavily. One of our suitcases shot across the floor of the cabin and the lights flickered and went out. There I was, crouched in the darkness, and for a few seconds completely terrified.

Thankfully the emergency lighting came on, but this was followed by another explosion. Strangely the ship appeared to right itself slightly more and I could stand up without holding on to anything. There followed a deadly silence, which was interrupted seconds later by children shouting for their mothers. There was so much noise and confusion. When the signal was given to abandon ship all hell broke loose.

I pulled on some trousers on top of my pyjamas, slipped into a pair of shoes and was just putting my lifejacket on when my parents turned up. They grabbed me and we headed off for the lifeboat station. Incredibly there were Polish guards with fixed bayonets holding back the Italian prisoners in order to let the women and children escape. On the stairs I bumped into a girl called Pamela, who I had got friendly with during the trip. She was looking for her father while a brave young airman attempted to fasten his 'Mae West' around her. I was startled to see a man – completely naked – trying to cover himself with his hands while trying to make his way up the stairs!

We reached the lifeboat station and climbed on to a rope ladder, but the boat went off without us and we were left dangling. It's strange, but up to this point everyone was following the drill like robots. I wasn't frightened – I was just automatically doing what I was told, going through a well-practised drill. Another boat pulled over. My father climbed on board and a man grabbed my right foot. The ladder swung away from the boat and there I was practically doing the splits on the side of the ship. In agony I let go and plunged down into the sea below. I was hauled out of the water (again by my foot) by an unknown seaman. My poor mother fell in head-first. There then began a mad splashing of oars and a concerted effort to get away from the sinking ship. We were worried that the boilers would explode and that we would be sucked down with her. To my horror, I noticed that there were still quite a number of people on board running about in panic. I got terribly seasick as I'd swallowed so much filthy sea water, so didn't actually see the ship sink. I know all the lights had gone out at some point, though. And of course you could still hear the screams. Just before the ship disappeared under the waves we heard the engines of a submarine as it passed us in the dark.

The next day, after passing the remainder of the night and morning in the lifeboat, we spotted the submarine. It was coming straight towards us. We were convinced that it was going to ram our lifeboat. The men were shouting and I just shut my eyes, put my head on my mother's lap and prayed and prayed, literally shaking with fear. To our amazement, instead of ramming us we felt only a small bump, after which a German officer appeared and apologised! They even gave us water, coffee, and tins of evaporated milk.

The next day another submarine arrived – U-507. We were fed hot soup and given more water. The Captain offered to take the women and children on board. He said it would be more comfortable for us. My mother and her friend Mrs Baker talked it over. She was travelling alone with her son and daughter and was, naturally, very frightened. One of the men said they'd probably shoot the men and rape the women and girls, so we refused to go. (Later we found out that the ones that did go had been well treated by their captors.)

We remained in that lifeboat for five days. On the last day the submarine returned and an officer told us that one of the submarines had been bombed by an American plane but we were to wait for a French boat, which would pick us up. It was very hot with very little water, rationed twice a day. Time meant nothing, but it had begun to cool a little when we saw a dot on the horizon, which turned out to be a Vichy French cruiser – the *Gloire*. The crew let down ladders and hauled us on board. Instantly we were given a hot drink with either rum or brandy in it. We were taken down to the ship's infirmary. The men were put into the holds and the women and children slept on the floor of a couple of officers' cabins.

It was simply unbearable to see the awful realisation on people's faces when they learned that their loved ones hadn't made it. I will never forget the sight of three small children who had lost both their parents. My friend Lucy had lost her mother and younger siblings. One mother had managed to save her three-year-old, but her husband and young son were both lost. Pamela's father was lucky, though. He thought he had lost her but they were re-united. The reason they had been making the trip was because his wife had died and Pamela was all he had. You can imagine the joy he felt when they were re-united. There were so many emotional scenes, tears, misery and relief. The ship sailed on to Casablanca and we were put into camps. The single men went to one, while family units were taken to an old Foreign Legion camp about 50 miles from Casablanca. We were now prisoners in Camp Sidi El Avanchi.

Conditions were grim. Food was scarce until eventually the American Consul finally received permission to visit. They brought much-needed clothing, which they had collected from Embassy families, and also porridge and milk for children under 16 and pregnant women. One of the young mothers who had been nursing her baby had had a terrible time in the lifeboat because her milk had dried up. Miraculously as soon as she was rescued it suddenly came back and the baby was able to suckle again. One morning we heard what sounded like gun fire in the distance. Later, we were confined to our quarters. Then an American plane flew over and the pilot waved. The guards tried to shoot at him with rifles. Next day the guns sounded even closer. By standing on my tip-toes on the toilet block I could just see the tanks getting nearer. The day after that the French flag was taken down and the guards vanished. Suddenly the gates were flung open and there stood an American Army officer. He was mobbed and everyone shouted with joy. Someone even played 'Yankee Doodle Dandy' and we all drank a toast to General Eisenhower. He asked the English families to accompany him to the commandant's house. He told us about the American and British African landing and said that arrangements would be made to get us home. We were given food and the men were able to indulge in a cigarette.

Soon after that we were put on to coaches – women and children only – and given a bar of chocolate each. We were driven to a hospital ship at Casablanca. I remember being able to have a bath and – wonder of wonders – white bread and butter! There was tea and cake, too – a veritable feast.

Next stop was Gibraltar and the colonial hospital. We were given more clothes, underwear and heavy naval greatcoats and nurse-issue shoes. Our next ship was the *Ormonde*, which brought us to Liverpool, this time in a convoy arriving a few days before Christmas 1942. The men arrived much later as they went via America. I started to have panic attacks on the *Ormonde* – a delayed reaction to the whole experience, I suppose. I'm not afraid of the sea, though, and have been on the odd cross-Channel ferry since then.

Although the circumstances were entirely different, watching the horror of the September 11th terrorist attack in New York brought back all the fears of seeing that U-boat coming towards us and not knowing whether we would live or die. That sort of feeling never leaves you.

CITY OF SIMLA
(1940)

12 April 2002

A welcome package in the post this morning containing a cassette tape with an oral account of Elizabeth Sladden's childhood memories of the *City of Simla*, which sank on 21 September 1940.

Somewhere at the bottom of the Atlantic Ocean, roughly 50 miles north-west of Malin Head, lies the humble wreck of the *City of Simla*. Unlike the *Titanic* there has never been a public obsession with her; nobody spends millions of pounds trying to salvage her or photograph her. She exists like a half-forgotten dream recalled only by the few who sailed on her. In the chronicle of maritime history she is afforded little more than a few lines of bare statistics.

Elizabeth Sladden was only a child of seven when she and her mother sailed on the *City of Simla* on its last journey. However, the memories of it readily come back to her, though they are not always welcome.

Up until the ship sank, Mrs Sladden told me that it was rather fun. The adults often took a different view. Actor and writer Noel Coward – who had travelled many times during the inter-war years on the *Titanic*'s sister ship, *Olympic* – didn't appreciate the presence of young children on one memorable war time crossing:

'On Sunday, July 21st, 1940, I sailed from Liverpool for New York on the *Britannic*. The ship, crammed to the gunwales, had been lying in the Mersey for twenty-four hours with several other large vessels until the convoy escort was ready to usher it onto the bosom of the Atlantic. Many of the passengers lived in their lifebelts and we queued for everything; meals were staggered because there were too many of us to be served at one sitting. We queued up not only for lunch and dinner but for baths, lavatories and even lifeboat drill. The ship was overrun by children ranging from babies a few months old to cheerful little boys of twelve and thirteen, who wore neat grey flannel suits, scampered up and down the decks chattering to each other in clear, treble English voices, and treated the whole voyage as a high adventure, which indeed it might have been. There were several play-pens put up on the promenade deck in which anxious mothers could deposit their younger offspring and snatch a few hours comparative peace. Fortunately the weather was calm, so there was no seasickness to contend with. However, from dawn to dusk the noise was ear-splitting. Only after dinner in the smoking room, when the young had been stowed away in their bunks, was it possible to be quiet and make believe for a little that it was an ordinary voyage without urgency and the underlying dread of disaster...'

The *City of Simla* was travelling as part of a large convoy from London to Bombay. On board were 350 passengers and crew under the care of Captain Herbert Percival. On 21 September 1940 she was torpedoed and sunk by U-138 with the loss of three lives. With so few survivors of the disaster alive today, Elizabeth Sladden's account is all the more precious.

ELIZABETH SLADDEN

66 Funny what you remember as a child, isn't it? My memories of the *City of Simla* are like a jigsaw with pieces missing. It's odd how I can hardly conjure up what the ship itself was like, as I suppose I had nothing to compare it to. It must have seemed huge to me, what with my being so young, but I guess you just accept things when you're that age and take them for granted. All I knew was that my mother and I were going to see my father who was away and it was terribly exciting. I was only seven years old at the time, and while some of it is rather hazy there are other points which I can recall with great clarity, as one does as a child.

My father was in the Indian Army. We were going out to Burma, destination Rangoon. We didn't actually have a home in England, although my grandparents were all from the North East of England. My mother and I set off together as my father had already gone ahead of us. We shared a very small cabin with bunk beds. I couldn't possibly tell you about the rest of the ship – another piece of the jigsaw gone for ever! I suppose it looked rather grand to me, but the subsequent events erased the memory of it entirely.

I was tucked up in bed asleep when the ship was attacked. I was in my nightclothes but my mother was fully dressed and I can recall vividly that she was wearing trousers and a shirt. She must have been up when the ship was torpedoed – or maybe she was just taking precautions in case we had to evacuate quickly. My mother's hands were shaking badly as she tried to tie the lifebelt around me. She grabbed me by the hand and together we rushed up a stairwell trying to get to the boat deck, and as we did a man stopped to help fix my lifebelt on properly, as my mother was obviously all fingers and thumbs by this point.

We next found ourselves in a lounge on the upper deck. There was a large curtain over the exit door and I can remember distinctly a man parting it and saying, 'Women and children first!' One word sprung into my head: *Titanic*! I didn't like that at all! We knew what lifeboat station to go to because we had had a drill earlier in the trip, so there was no confusion about that. However, when we got there we discovered to our horror that the boat was missing and we were told to find another one. In fact, all the lifeboats had been lowered by this point. That sense of utter panic and bewilderment comes back to me as strongly today as all those years ago.

You must remember that it was dark and we were far out to sea at this point. The water didn't look terribly inviting to me and I know my mother was worried sick. We had to climb down a rope ladder to a lifeboat which was standing by. Someone was holding it steady and every time there was a swell you had to make a jump for it in order to get in. I didn't like that much! I seem to recall that some of the Indian Laskers – who had been serving on the ship – were held back by members of the crew as in their terror they had tried to get into the lifeboats before the women and children. Many years later I remember going to London with my mother and as we passed Selfridges she said that getting off the *City of Simla* that night would be like climbing down the side of the department store on a rope ladder in a strong wind.

A lady in the lifeboat was very distressed. She kept pointing accusingly at my mother asking why she was lucky enough to have me because her son, who had been sleeping in the cabin at the time of the attack, had been killed. I felt guilty, though I don't know why. You never argued with an adult in those days – you just had to accept what they said and keep quiet. None the less, even with my mother nearby it was a terribly uncomfortable time. That lady's hair turned completely white over the few hours that we were in the lifeboat. It was fascinating and unsettling all at once to look at her. Somebody on board got us all to say the Lord's Prayer, and later on we sang songs to keep our spirits up. We were rescued by a cargo ship which contained aeroplane parts. The captain was later relieved of his command because he had stopped in mid-ocean to pick up survivors, which went against wartime conventions as he was putting his own vessel in danger in order to do so.

We were taken aboard shortly before daybreak so we must have only been in the water for a few hours – although it seemed a lot longer than that, of course. Another rope ladder appeared over the side of the ship and we had to climb up. As I reached the deck level, two sailors hoisted me over and one of them put his coat around me. I was terrified because the next person after me wasn't my mother and I panicked. Where could she have got to? I was held back by the sailors who told me that they had to get all the children up first, and after that my mother would be the next adult. A pair of twin babies came next – hoisted up in a wooden rope sling. Eventually, of course, she appeared and we were taken to a cargo hold to rest. Since all of us children were in nightclothes, the sailors kindly gave us their thick white socks to wear so that we could run about on deck without hurting our feet! We played about as if nothing in the world had ever happened.

The ship made its way back to Gourock in Scotland and we were met by the Red Cross, who gave us money and clothes. We were then able to get back to my grandparents' house in Tynemouth. We weren't allowed to ring them and tell them because of the 'Careless talk costs lives' campaign. It was only when we got to Newcastle that my mother was allowed to contact them to let them know we were coming home – reason not specified. I must have looked quite a sight in a brown skirt and shoes with a flap that went over the laces. We did eventually get to India, but it wasn't until September 1945. We were actually travelling there when we heard the news of VJ Day.

Four years ago I went to Liverpool to the Battle of the Atlantic exhibition to find out a little more about the *City of Simla*. On getting out of the lift I was confronted with a huge screen with images of an angry sea heaving up and down. It was so shocking that instinctively I stepped back into the lift – all those feelings of terror coming back instantly. I was surprised at how I had reacted since it had been nearly sixty years since the disaster and I thought I'd put all those feelings behind me. The exhibition moved me deeply. However, I'm afraid I haven't been able to bring myself to watch the film *Titanic*. While I do love swimming, I'm still rather nervous of deep water.

Titanic threads...

Pat O'Keefe

'They say there was no moon the night *Titanic* sank,' says John Nolan. 'On chilly moonless nights I look up at the stars and think of my great-uncle. I shiver as I wonder, "What if I had to jump into the middle of the ocean right now? What if I was faced with a situation where I knew I was going to die?" You can't think about *Titanic* without thinking about death.'

As a man with Irish blood coursing through his veins, I've always loved hearing a good story (and telling the odd one, too!). I love stories like this. John Nolan wanted to find out more about his great-uncle, who had been a *Titanic* survivor. The story had circulated in his family for years but, being a natural sceptic, he wasn't sure where myth ended and reality began. In the late 1990s, with 'Titanic Fever' at its height due to the James Cameron film, he decided to do something about it.

The search for the facts went on for years. It is a tale that many an amateur genealogist would recognise. John wrote it all down in a charming book called *In Search of Great Uncle Pat, Titanic Survivor*. I read it from cover to cover within a few hours and was hooked by the trials, frustrations and personal triumphs the author experienced. It's a real adventure told with great warmth. I was also very moved by the story of Great Uncle Pat, and contacted his nephew to see if he would mind my telling it here. He quickly responded, saying that he would be delighted.

The night before he boarded the *Titanic* at Queenstown (now Cobh), Ireland, to seek his fortune in America, young Pat O'Keefe had a nightmare in which he saw the *Titanic* going down in the middle of the ocean. The 22-year-old Irish lad 'thought of selling his ticket the next day,' says John Nolan, 'but didn't want to go back to Waterford and have all his friends laughing at him.' He reluctantly put his premonition to one side and headed off with high hopes of a better life waiting for him on the other side of the Atlantic. Was it the luck of the Irish that saw him through the calamity?

'Being a steerage passenger, Pat was housed in a cabin on one of the lower decks, very likely in the bow section where most single men were bunked in groups, so he was probably immediately aware of the impact when *Titanic* struck the iceberg. When Pat went up top to see what was the matter, he was assured by a steward that it was nothing serious and he was advised to return to his cabin. Meanwhile, the lifeboats were being uncovered and first class passengers were quietly being told to put on their lifebelts and go to the boat deck.

When Pat returned to his cabin, he learned about the water coming into the ship, and he went back up. The lifeboats were being filled and Pat was now told to go back to his cabin and get his lifebelt. When he tried to do that, he found his cabin was filling up with water. With no lifebelt, he went up to the third class general room or smoking room, located on C deck at the stern, and watched the last of the lifeboats row away. He met two other third class passengers, Victor Sunderland and Edward Dorking, both from England, and they decided to jump from the steerage deck as the ocean washed over the forward end of the ship and the stern began to rise.

Pat swam away from the ship's side and came upon a "raft", as he called it. It turned out to be the overturned lifeboat Collapsible B. The boat had flipped over as crew members hurriedly tried to launch it from the rapidly sinking ship. Some crew members had managed to climb on to it as it floated off the ship, but they were knocked off when the forward funnel collapsed and smacked the water, sending the overturned boat away from the ship.

After climbing on to it, Pat pulled two other men on board, and the three of them paddled around, picking up others, including Sunderland and Dorking.'

Pat helped to haul in a number of other swimmers, but after a while the men were forced to make the agonising decision of turning others away. Their small boat would surely be swamped by the multitudes left behind in the water as the *Titanic* disappeared from sight. It was a matter of life or death now.

'Once they were away, someone on the upturned boat suggested that they pray. Each man called out his religion and they agreed to say the Lord's Prayer. Officer Lightoller [who had also managed to scramble on board] organised the men in standing positions to keep the boat balanced, and in the morning light he could see the other lifeboats and signalled with his whistle.'

The men were eventually picked up by the rescue ship *Carpathia* after spending hours wearing their sodden clothes, crisp now with frost, and bodily perished with blue limbs and numb fingers.

Father Michael Kenny, a New York Catholic priest who visited survivors at St Vincent's Hospital, was told that Pat O'Keefe was a hero and helped to pull people on to the overturned boat. Father Kenny was also told that several women made it to the collapsible, but no ladies were rescued from the overturned boat when morning came. If women did make it to the boat they did not last the night after being in the freezing water. Pat O'Keefe was only offered a free passage back to Queenstown on a White Star ship by way of compensation. He refused the offer and settled in America, never to return to his homeland. Tragically, he died of a massive heart attack at the relatively early age of 49 on 16 December 1939. For his wife Anna and two children, Margaret and Edward, it was a sad Christmas indeed.

Pat O'Keefe never had the chance to tell his son about the *Titanic*. Apparently he was putting it off until the boy was old enough to understand, but his own death put an end to it. What moves me about John Nolan's story is that in Pat O'Keefe we can surely trace the fate of any number of immigrants who boarded the *Titanic* and survived. It is sad to see how shabbily some of them were treated after the disaster and how easily fobbed off they were with pitiful amounts of remuneration by the White Star Line. However, it seems that for many, getting to America was a dream realised – no matter how tumultuous the journey – and they were grateful at least for that.

Harold Nicholson on Chips Channon

'1936: Chips is not really a snob in an ordinary way. I suppose everyone has some snobbishness somewhere just like everybody has a few keys somewhere.

What makes Chips so exceptional is that he collects keys for keys' sake. The corridors of his mind are hung with keys which open no doors of his own but are just other people's keys which he collects. There they hang – French keys, English keys, American keys, Italian keys and now a whole housekeeper's truss of General European keys.'

What, I wonder, would Mr Nicholson have made of my preoccupation with the *Titanic* and collecting shipwreck 'survivor keys'? Does it make me a survivor snob?

CITY OF CAIRO
(1942)

14 April 2002

A letter arrived all the way from Australia today. Apparently the advert I put in *Women's Weekly* last year has found its way to Birkdale, Queensland! John Martin survived the sinking of the *City of Cairo* and has written to ask me if I would like his account of what happened to him. Having read it through I'm delighted to include it here. I shall add it to another testimony I received this month from John Vass Morris, who was persuaded to commit his thoughts to paper by his granddaughter especially for me. Between them, Mr Morris and Mr Martin spent 19 days at sea in an open boat waiting to be rescued after the *City of Cairo* sank.

The Ellerman Line ship *City of Cairo* was another casualty of U-boat aggression. Built in 1915, it was sunk by a torpedo on 6 November 1942 while sailing from Bombay and Cape Town to Brazil en route to the United Kingdom. Relatively speaking John Martin and Jason Vass Morris were lucky. One lifeboat and its four survivors drifted on the open sea for a staggering 51 days before they were rescued.

However, survivors bore witness to an example of old Teutonic good breeding when, upon surfacing, U-boat commander Karl-Friedrich Merten – who had holed their ship – not only wished his victims well, but also gave them directions to the nearest safe haven! Perhaps he simply wanted to give them a fighting chance? Maritime historian Ralph Barker expressed the oddity of this encounter at sea in the title of his detailed account of the disaster, *Goodnight, sorry for sinking you!*, published 20 years ago.

JOHN MARTIN

❝ I was a Royal Navy Gunner and joined the *City of Cairo* around May or June 1942 in Glasgow. Gunners were treated as crew members and I was in a cabin with three other naval ratings amidships. It was pretty comfortable and I had no complaints. We had our own mess deck where he had our meals. A lot of our spare time was spent there playing cards, reading or making whatever entertainment we could.

While the ship was at sea we kept look-out watches for enemy aircraft, ships or submarines, doing four hours on and eight hours off continuously.

When we were attacked I was in another gunner's cabin and had to find a way back to my own cabin to find my own lifejacket. Unfortunately, the lifeboat I was in (No 7) was pretty badly damaged, with the rudder smashed to pieces and the water leaking, as the second torpedo exploded pretty close to it.

The U-boat surfaced and was in amongst the lifeboats and asked for the Captain of the *Cairo*, but he was told that the latter had gone down with the ship. The Captain of the U-boat gave us a course to steer for St Helena, and that we were around 400 miles from there. Then he said, 'Goodnight, sorry for sinking you,' and left.

Three young seaman gunners and myself rowed as much as possible for three or four days until we struck bad weather and our hands were badly blistered. The water we had on board was rationed of course and we only had an eggcupful or two ounces twice a day. We were also given beef extract and some awful chocolate and malted milk biscuits, which made you very dry.

We ran into bad weather with wild and windy storms for several days, but there was absolutely no rain. By then several people had died – mostly Indian crew members – which meant we had to get them into the sea where sharks continuously followed. The weather also caused the lifeboats to get split up. Fortunately boat No 5 and our boat No 7 managed to stay together. Somebody was able to use the sextant, and since another chap had a decent watch we had a fair idea of how far away we were from St Helena. Luckily we didn't have to row the whole way there because we were eventually spotted – but it took quite some time for help to come. The *Titanic* survivors only had to wait a few hours for rescue. We had six days in that lifeboat!

Naturally, reaching St Helena was wonderful for all of us as we were carted off to hospital for a week and then were sent back to Cape Town for three weeks' leave at a little place called Somerset West. A real luxury indeed!

JOHN VASS MORRIS

❝ I joined the Royal Navy in 1942 when I was 19 years old. After my 20th birthday in May I was stationed on the *City of Cairo* as one of four seamen gunners.

After we left Cape Town we were ordered to leave our convoy and alter course and go to Pernambucco, Brazil, to collect passengers there and return them to the UK. This was risky as, without any protection, we were very exposed – and so it proved.

Millvina Dean, aged about 2, not long after surviving the sinking of the *Titanic* (*above left*), and as a young woman in about 1930.

In 1940 *City of Benares* was torpedoed, but 11-year-old 'seavacuee' Colin Ryder Richardson escaped. 'It changed everything for me, more so than perhaps I realised at the time and not for the better,' he says.

Above As a 35-year-old science teacher Lawrence Beesley sailed to New York on the *Titanic*, later writing an account of his experiences. He is seen here (left) at a reunion at Caius College, Cambridge, in the 1950s.

Above right Beesley's daughter Dinah Quilter told the author her father's story. As a child she would pore over his acrapbook trying to imagine what it had been like for him. 'He had an aversion to the sea for the rest of his life.'

Joanna Spreckley (right) served as a VAD in the First World War. 'I remember rushing into the house calling out to my parents that I had heard the newsboy say that the *Titanic* had sunk. No one would believe it.'

Only just over a quarter of the children on board the *Lusitania* survived when it was infamously torpedoed in 1915; Audrey Pearl (*above left*) and her older brother Stuart were very lucky, but they lost their sisters Amy and Susan. Their mother, Amy Lea Pearl (*right*), also survived, as did their father, Major Warren Pearl. Today Audrey actively supports the RNLI to honour her mother's memory.

Above As a young man Roy Leadbetter (second from left, back row) craved adventure, and found it when he managed to escape with his life when the *Rawalpindi* sank on 23 November 1939.

Left The entire course of Elizabeth Dunn's life changed after she survived the sinking of the *City of Nagpur* in 1941.

Above The *Titanic* disaster robbed Ellen Mary Walker of a father and denied her the love, care and support of her mother Kate, with whom she is seen here shortly after the disaster. 'The only thing the *Titanic* has ever meant to me is sorrow,' she says. 'Quite simply, it has ruined most of my life.'

Below Audrey Tiller survived the torpedoing of the Cunard liner *Laconia* in September 1942, although many subsequent victims would be less fortunate following the issuing of Dönitz's infamous 'Laconia Order', forbidding German vessels from rescuing any Allied survivors at sea.

Below Elizabeth Sladden was only a child of seven when she and her mother sailed on the *City of Simla* on its last journey in 1940.

Between them, John Vass Morris (*left*) and John Martin spent 19 days at sea in an open boat waiting to be rescued after the *City of Cairo* was torpedoed in 1942. 'Goodnight, sorry for sinking you,' were the parting words of the U-boat Captain when he surfaced after sinking their ship.

Left Leonard Jones joined the *Empress of Britain* on 7 March 1940 as a Cabin Steward, and survived the loss of the ship towards the end of its voyage home from Cape Town.

Right Kathleen Preston and her husband, seen here on their wedding day, were relieved to get a passage home to Britain from South Africa in 1940. Together with hundreds of other expatriates, they thought it was fortuitous to be booked on the *Empress of Britain*, until she was bombed and set alight off the north-west coast of Ireland, the largest British merchant vessel to be sunk in the Second World War.

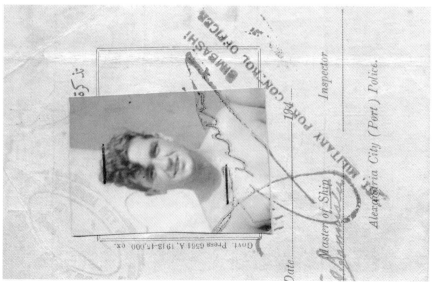

Susan Moss (*above left*) was pregnant with her daughter Margaret (*above right*) when the *Titanic* sank. Her husband William Moss, a first class saloon steward aboard the liner, perished, aged 34. He is seen here (*below left*) on the extreme right with the *Olympic*'s crew cricket team in 1911. 'After my father died, my mother's life become one big financial struggle,' recalls Margaret.

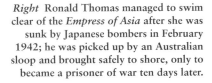

Right Ronald Thomas managed to swim clear of the *Empress of Asia* after she was sunk by Japanese bombers in February 1942; he was picked up by an Australian sloop and brought safely to shore, only to became a prisoner of war ten days later.

After leaving the convoy, we steamed our way at ten knots towards our destination when we were suddenly attacked without warning by a German U-boat firing at us with the first of two torpedoes, which went into the fore of the ship. This was around 9pm, then after another twenty minutes the second torpedo was fired, which went into the engine room.

I was fortunate to escape before the second torpedo hit. People were scrambling to get to the lifeboats, but two of them had been shattered by the blast and the remaining six lifeboats were overloaded while two were severely damaged.

I, along with other Army personnel, Merchant Navy crew plus my Royal Navy shipmates, were scrambling to get through a hole that had been cut out in the cabin door. I managed to escape through the hole wearing just a pair of shorts and white shoes. Realising I had no lifebelt, I went back into the cabin and collected one. On my way back to the deck below, the connecting ladder had been blown away and I fell about ten feet on to the deck below. I landed face down and bruised my ankle, but I managed to get up and find my way to the lifeboat station.

I climbed on to lifeboat 8, which mostly contained first class passengers. There were also six babies, some young children and crew. We quickly got the oars out and rowed away from the sinking ship. Just at this moment the second torpedo fired and the *City of Cairo* broke in half and sank.

The Coxswain wanted to tie all the lifeboats together in order to keep all the survivors in sight of each other, but before this happened the U-boat surfaced alongside us. The German Captain wanted to know where our Captain was – plus the whereabouts of any other officers who may have survived. Our Captain was floating on a raft somewhere and could not be located. The U-boat Captain asked us what cargo we had been carrying, where we were bound and where we had come from. He appeared satisfied with the information we gave him and then, in an effort to put us on course, he told us that we were 1,000 miles from Walvis Bay and 500 miles from St Helena island. After he pointed out the way to St Helena he prepared to leave. He turned around and said, 'Goodnight, sorry for sinking you. I was only doing my duty.' And with that, the U-boat disappeared beneath the waves.

Somehow we got separated from the other lifeboats and by the next day there were no other people to be seen.

During my time in the lifeboat myself and some of the crew managed to go swimming around the boat (even though the waters were shark-infested) while the other shipmates kept a lookout. The women and children on board were given the blankets and all I had was my lifejacket, a pair of shorts and white shoes. During the day the weather used to get very hot, so I and my fellow shipmates suffered with sunburn. During the night it was extremely cold and there were often times when I thought we were never going to make it. The rations were distributed twice daily. A bottle of brandy was opened and was given to one of the engineers who had been seriously hurt. Most of the time we were sat in water and we had to bail out constantly.

There were two Indian seamen who used to drink salt water. One night, after drinking a lot of water, one of them jumped over the side. The Coxswain immediately turned the boat around and he was pulled back into the boat. He then warned the other Indian seaman that if they decided to do the same he would not be rescued as there were 75 other people on the lifeboat and he was not prepared to put their lives at risk.

However, another Indian seaman jumped overboard after drinking salt water, which must have turned him crazy. It happened during the night and he was not rescued. The rest of the Indian seamen – which were known as Laskers – accused the lifeboat crew of drinking the fresh water at night, so the Coxswain immediately ordered two of the most senior crew to guard the barrel of water on night duty.

During the first week a blanket was held up by two Matelots for the benefit of the women on board in order to preserve their dignity.

On the morning of our thirteenth day at sea a man who had been a passenger aboard the ship wearing a monocle stood up by the mast. He alerted the Coxswain to what he thought was a cloud on the horizon. However, the Coxswain, realising it was land, said, 'We will make it to St Helena by nightfall!'

Before we got there we were spotted and picked up by a clam boat called the *Clan McAlpine*, which already had survivors on board from the previous day. After being at sea in an open boat for thirteen days it was a welcome sight. Their crew appeared to be over the moon to see us – a feeling we all shared!

After our ordeal we were exhausted and were immediately given medical treatment by the ship's doctor, but very little food except for Cape oranges, bread and butter. We were made very comfortable on the deck of the ship. Later that day, from St Helena we were sent to various hospitals around the island. I was sent to a small Army hospital as I was unable to walk because my feet were swollen with the salt water. After a few days I was gradually re-introduced to more substantial food and was given my choice of the full menu, which was wonderful.

EMPRESS OF BRITAIN
(1940)

22 June 2002

I'm so glad that Kathleen Preston and Leonard Jones decided to get in touch with me. I didn't feel this collection would be complete without a mention of the beautiful ship the *Empress of Britain* and its sad demise on 26 October 1940. Now I have not one but two fascinating accounts in my possession.

To sail on the *Empress of Britain* during the inter-war years must have been a delightful experience. Built in 1931, she was the largest ship ever constructed for the Canadian Pacific Line's Southampton-Quebec service. At 42,350 tons and with her three mighty funnels, she would have appeared more than a little majestic to the casual observer.

The *Empress of Britain* was impressive enough to be given the Royal seal of approval when King George VI and Queen Elizabeth chose to travel on her for their return journey from Canada on a state visit in June 1939. The Second World War was to alter her status to more functional purposes when she was taken over by the Admiralty as a troopship. Conditions on board changed quite dramatically, as the 26-year-old Countess of Ranfurly found on 28 September 1940. In her diary she wrote:

> 'This is Hades. We are clamped down below decks because we are passing enemy territory... The heat is unbelievable. The swimming pool has been emptied for this perilous period. At midday, when the bar opens, the rush for it is astonishing. Toby says we're in a floating inebriates' home. The officer commanding troops confided in me today that the lower decks are fast turning into a brothel. He has had to post sentries to try to restore order... Quite a lot of people are "enjoying the voyage"...'

Our story begins one month later as the *Empress of Britain* prepared to make the return journey from South Africa to the UK.

Kathleen Preston told me that she and her husband were simply relieved to have been granted a passage to get them back home. Together with hundreds of other expatriates, they thought it was fortuitous to be booked on to the *Empress of Britain*. Surely nothing could happen to such a sturdy-looking ship? Perhaps Cabin Steward Leonard Jones reassured Mr and Mrs Preston as he went about his duties. He was pretty new to the ship himself, having only joined her three months before. But he knew his job well and tried to make his charges feel as comfortable as possible. No doubt the passengers made good use of the (limited) amenities on board and enjoyed the unrationed food. Mrs Preston says in her letter that as they got closer to their destination, the most people could honestly say about the trip was that, all in all, it had been both pleasant and mercifully uneventful.

This situation was to drastically change on 26 October as the *Empress of Britain* neared the north-west coast of Ireland. Without warning she was attacked by German bombers using high explosives and incendiary bombs, which soon set her ablaze. As if determined not to suffer such an ignominious end, the ship stubbornly remained afloat and was taken in tow by the Polish destroyer *Burza*. It made her easy prey for submarine aggression and almost inevitably two days later she was torpedoed and sunk by U-32.

There were an estimated 45 to 50 fatalities between the two attacks on the *Empress of Britain*. Furthermore, to this ship goes the dubious distinction of being the largest British merchant vessel to be sunk in the Second World War.

When he contacted me last week, Leonard Jones made no mention of how he had made his escape from the stricken liner. However, today I received a press cutting from him that speaks for itself. An all but forgotten hero.

KATHLEEN PRESTON

66 As the German forces in 1940 were gathering momentum in their approach to Alexandria, all British families were evacuated either to Palestine or South Africa (Durban). I was teaching in the Garrison School, Abbassinia, near Cairo at the time while my husband was serving with the Royal Engineers. I was also expecting our first child. My husband was ordered home to the UK, which therefore required us to continue in the *Empress of Britain* after landing the other families in Durban.

We proceeded by rail from Cairo to Suez, where several ships were anchored. We were transferred by lighter and taken on board by a very surprised crew, who were evidently not expecting us. Assembled in a lounge, we were just in time to hear the local six o'clock news, which informed us that the *Empress of Britain* had been torpedoed and sunk by a German U-boat! We smiled – a bit too soon. Husbands and wives were separated and allotted cabins or beds in large dormitories, and soon we were on our way down to Durban. The voyage was uneventful and free from worry. My husband and I were given a state room, with real beds, not bunks, but I was provided with brushes and dusters and required to keep it clean. The food, however, was good, although I lived mostly on toast and hot Marmite drinks.

On board, as a teacher, I was expected to occupy some of the children. I cannot remember anything I tried to teach. We had a ship's concert, of which I remember only 'South of the Border, Down Mexico Way', and a very disgruntled crew member threatening to withdraw his display of 'Playing the Spoons' if he was refused a better place in the billing.

We had a day or two at Durban and a welcome spell on dry land, but I cannot remember much of the countryside, only the huge black man who pulled us around in his rickshaw. Next stop was Cape Town, and several days enjoying some sight-seeing before facing the ordeal of several weeks zigzagging up the mid-Atlantic. I remember standing at a high viewpoint in Cape Town and gazing down at the *Empress* anchored in Table Bay and simply dreading the moment when we should have to re-embark. Something about it sent a shiver down my spine, though for the life of me I couldn't think why.

Everything was quite ordinary until we were off the north-west coast of Ireland. On the morning of 21 October we had put on warm clothing in readiness for landing in Scotland, and we were taking some exercise, walking around the promenade deck, chatting about this and that, when a small plane appeared.

'Oh, look!' someone said, 'Our escort come to see us safely into port.'

'How do your know it's an escort?' I asked. But before there was time to reply a bomb fell amidships and part of the ship's side disappeared – as did my hat and scarf.

We fell to the deck, but a Naval Petty Officer came and lifted me up. My husband got to his feet and we fled aft. It was terrifying. However, everybody quietly went about doing what we had been told to do. Three or four bombs were dropped, fierce fires broke out and then the plane flew away. We were guided to the ship's side, where lifeboats were being lowered. The men set about getting us into the lifeboats, helping us over the side and encouraging us to hold tight.

At first we were encouraged to lower ourselves by clinging to flattened hoses, but eventually ropes were found and I began the descent, unable to see a boat, and wondering how long I could hold my own weight. I lost sight of my husband, but just as our boat was about to move off, fully laden, he appeared. Many of the women slid down and arrived at the bottom with hands torn and bleeding. I was lucky. We were rowed around for an hour or two while the ship burned and ammunition exploded all around.

I sat in the boat thankful to be alive, but I couldn't help thinking about my lovely trousseau, which was gone forever, together with our most treasured possessions, which we thought would be safer with us than travelling by cargo ship with our boxes. (The boxes arrived months later full of broken vases and articles I could really have done without. Later I felt guilty in having wasted valuable space in a transport ship plying the seas in those perilous times.) Eventually we saw smoke on the horizon and HMS *Echo* picked us up. The women were put into the Captain's cabins and we were given hot water bottles (actually beer bottles) to warm us up, and corned beef hash produced like magic by the jolly Jack Tars. On landing at Greenock on the Clyde, we were surrounded by help on every side; we were taken to a clothing depot and fitted out with any clothes we wanted, then put up for a few nights at the Central Hotel, in great comfort. After this we made our way by train to Gosport where my husband awaited his orders – which took us both back to Scotland and eventually a new life. The *Empress of Britain* disaster then became a rather distant memory. However, I can appreciate a little of what happened on the *Titanic* now!

I am amazed that it never entered my head that either the *Empress* or the lifeboat, or HMS *Echo*, would be in any danger. I also feel very lucky to have suffered so little from the experience. I wonder sometimes what happened to the Naval Petty Officer who was so kind to me. I shall probably never know.

LEONARD JONES

Havant Survivor of Bombed Liner

Looking little worse after his terrible ordeal on the bombed liner *Empress of Britain*, steward Leonard George Jones (18), younger son of Mr and Mrs T. Jones, of 2 Selbourne Road, Havant, has arrived home.

He told an *Evening News* representative:

'I heard an air raid warning. Immediately afterwards there was a terrific crash – a bomb had exploded in the saloon.

'I had left my life-saving jacket on a chair in the saloon, and luckily, when I rushed back,. I found it in the same place.

'The staircase had been blown away. I managed to find an alternative way out and got on to E deck where I helped to close the watertight door.

'Amid all the alarm and peril we heard quite a lot of humour. The crockery man, for instance, noticing the plates all smashed, said, "Well, I can blame it all on the air raid."

'The top deck was ablaze, but everyone went to his post calmly and we all helped older people, women and children into the lifeboats.

'The fire hose was slung over the side of the ship and many slid down into the lifeboats. I got down with a little girl above me so that if she lost her hold I would be near enough to help her.

'Her mother let go of the hose as her hands got scorched and fell into the lifeboat but her elder daughter was drowned. I believe this was the only fatality among the women passengers.

'As we rowed round picking up people in the sea, humour was still rife, even among those struggling for life.

'One chap cried, "I can't swim!" His mate retorted, "Well, now is your chance to learn," but he accompanied this remark with a helping hand and got him into the boat.

Jones paid tribute to the ship's doctor. 'He worked like a hero,' he said, 'and amputated injured limbs while the lifeboat was tossing about in the heavy seas. 'The chief gunlayer, who I believe is a Portsmouth man, received a broken arm.' Jones said that he used to have a figure of Buddha as a mascot, but was told by a friend that it was unlucky to carry it about so he got rid of it just before the liner set out on its last trip.

❝ I was actually born in Havant, so I was a local lad made good I suppose! I started work at fourteen in the grocery trade until my eighteenth birthday. My father was already at sea and gave me the chance to join the *Empress of Australia*, sailing under the Canadian Pacific flag. My first trip was as an engineer's boy – a bit grubby to say the least – on 21 January 1939. It was cruising to South America and the Mediterranean. By May I was in very high company as on a trip to Quebec the King and Queen were on board.

In September we were on government charter, which meant a change of ship for me to the *Empress of Britain*. I joined her on 7 March 1940 as a Cabin Steward. That all came to an end when we were sailing back from Cape Town on 26 October 1940, when we where bombed and torpedoed. It was pretty rough but you just had to get on with it. I've never seen any of the crew since then as we were a mixed lot from all over the country, not like the Navy where crews were kept together.

I went back to Southampton as I was now under the Merchant Navy and sailed on a number of fine ships like the *Aquitania*, the *Queen Mary* and the *Carnarvon Castle*. Unbelievably, lightning struck twice when I took part in the invasion of France. The ship I was travelling on – the *Empire Javelin* – was torpedoed as we made our way there on 28 December 1944. But that's another story.

The most tragic thing I ever witnessed came a little later when I sailed on the *Almanzora* to pick up men from the Japanese prison camps in Singapore. A very sorry sight to see indeed.

Later on after the war I did another spell on the *Aquitania* – this time taking war brides over to the USA. It wasn't very pleasant for them and they were treated rather badly. Like the troops, they slept in bunks two and three high. Many had small children with them and had never sailed before. You had to feel sorry for the poor things. Most of them had no idea what to expect when they arrived in America and I often wonder what became of them.

Having had enough of deep-sea life I joined the Southern Railway on the Brittany run crossing to Jersey and St Malo until, after eleven years, I finished with the sea altogether and joined the local water company in 1950. I suppose I went from salt water to fresh water. It was a much more peaceful way of life after all my adventures, I can assure you!

Titanic threads...
Margaret Moss

I f I've learned anything while researching for this diary it's to expect the unexpected. Margaret Moss punctuates her conversation with peals of laughter even when she's talking about the *Titanic*. It's not that she is in any way unreverential about it – quite the opposite. I think it's the natural 'joie de vivre' in her character, and partly because she, like Millvina Dean, just can't believe all the fuss that is made of her nowadays (after a life of anonymity) when she attends exhibition openings and the like. I rather think she secretly enjoys it, and why not? As one of '*Titanic*'s daughters' she certainly didn't have an easy start in life.

'When I was very young a lady used to often come and visit us. My mother would dress my sister and I in our Sunday best and we were told to sit quietly and behave. I never knew what the lady wanted until I was old enough to understand about the *Titanic*. She was from the Titanic Relief Fund and would make three of four visits a year to check up on us and to make sure my mother hadn't remarried. If she had, the fund would have stopped paying her pension. As it was we barely had enough to live on, but my mother Susan was a proud Scottish woman and missed many a meal so that my older sister Elizabeth and I wouldn't go without.

My father, William Moss, was a first class saloon steward on the *Titanic* and died in the wreck, aged 34. If his body was found it was never identified, so there is no grave. But I've often wondered what his life was like aboard those great ships.'

A man like William Moss would have had his work cut out for him from the moment the *Titanic* left Southampton:

'For a dining room steward, the day began at 6.00am when he stumbled out of his bunk in one of the big dormitories on E deck, donned his saloon steward's uniform then headed back to the dining room to set up for breakfast. There was little time for rest in a steward's long day. When not actually working in the dining area, he could usually be found assisting one of the other public room stewards, perhaps serving

beef broth on deck or assisting with afternoon tea. If he was lucky, he might catch forty winks in the late afternoon before it was time to set up for dinner. But he would be grateful to be in bed before midnight.'
    Last Dinner on the Titanic, Archbold and McCauley

In *A Night to Remember*, Walter Lord describes the scene in the first class dining saloon as the *Titanic* brushed past the iceberg. Perhaps William Moss was one of those present?

'Meanwhile, down in the first class dining saloon on D deck, four other members of the *Titanic*'s crew were sitting round one of the tables. The last diner had long since departed, and now the big white Jacobean room was empty except for this single group. They were dining room stewards, indulging in that time-honoured pastime of all stewards off duty – they were gossiping about their passengers. Then, as they sat there talking, a faint grinding jar seemed to come from somewhere deep inside the ship. It was not much, but enough to break the conversation and rattle the silver that was set for breakfast next morning...'

Lord gives us a tantalising glimpse of William Moss as he and steward George Dodd attempted to rouse their fellow crew members and see for themselves the damage the impact had caused:

'Dodd moved forward to the waiters' quarters, where saloon steward William Moss was trying to rouse the men. Most of them were laughing and joking when Dodd burst in, shouting, "Get every man up! Don't let a man stay here!"
    He moved on with Moss towards the stewards' quarters. Just outside, smoking room steward [James] Witter was already getting some disturbing news from carpenter Hutchinson: "The bloody mail room is full." Moss came up and added, "It's really serious, Jim."'

After that, we can only speculate as to what William Moss did in those last few hours before the end came. Margaret continues:

'My mother was already pregnant with me when the *Titanic* sank and I was born four months later. My father had worked for the White Star Line for a number of years and had already served on the *Olympic*.
    After my father died, my mother's life become one big financial struggle. The money from the Titanic Relief Fund helped, of course. They gave her about £5 a month, but it certainly wasn't enough to feed and clothe my sister and me. Consequently, she took in boarders to augment her income. In every way she put us first. I'm sure that's why she never remarried and, being Scottish, she kept things to herself. Naturally she told us what happened to our father when she felt the time was right, but it wasn't something she dwelt on.

Being reasonably clever, my mother wanted me to stay on at school. I then went to college and took a shorthand, book-keeping and typing course. As a result I got a good job as a secretary. She was determined that we should make the most of ourselves. However, the *Titanic* and the struggles my mother faced afterwards all took their toll. She didn't enjoy good health and died of cancer quite young. Although the fund helped us financially, people were far less inclined to give in to their emotions in those days. You just had to toughen up.

Once I was older I used to think of the *Titanic* and wonder what life would have been like if my father had lived. I doubt I would have stayed in Scotland. His brothers and family lived in Bristol and I still keep in touch with one of my cousins there. Many of my cousins went to sea, so I think it must be in the blood. My older sister is still alive too so we're certainly a hardy lot!

A few years ago I was invited by the Falkirk Titanic Society to the opening of an exhibition in Stirling, which was very interesting. I've read a number of books about the *Titanic* and over the years have seen various films on the subject. When I attended the exhibition all sorts of people wanted to talk to me about it, which I was delighted to do. But the wreck of the *Titanic* should be left in peace – the thought of people rooting around inside the ship is dreadful. After all, it's a memorial to the dead – including my father.

After my mother died, we found a letter amongst her possessions which my father had written to her aboard the *Titanic* a month before it sank. He was on board when the ship was in Belfast – no doubt trying to get himself accustomed to his new surroundings. It's full of concern for mother and Elizabeth – just a quick scribble really. I'll send you a copy if you like.'

And that's just what she did. I think the PS is especially poignant:

'SS Titanic
Belfast
March 30/1912

My darling wife

Just a few lines to say I received your kind letter safely and am pleased that you and the wee bairn are in the best of health ... money [his wages] goes in first of the month. With heaps of love and kisses I remain your loving hubby,

Will
xxxxxxxxx
xxxxxxxxx

PS Do not write as I shan't be able to get it.'

EMPRESS OF ASIA
(1942)

28 June 2002

A photograph in the mail this morning. Sixty years ago a young soldier sat for his portrait and here he was smiling back at me. When I flipped it over I saw the name Ronald Thomas neatly inscribed on the rough cardboard backing. I was so glad to be able to put a face to the name of a man I had come to admire and respect so much.

In March 1960 the last vestiges of the mighty ocean liner *Empress of Asia* were being picked over for scrap near the Sultan Shoal just west of Keppel Harbour. A surprising discovery, perhaps. Nevertheless, it was here, in this unlikely graveyard, that the *Empress of Asia* ended her days, burnt out and grounded eighteen years before.

The Canadian Pacific's *Empress of Asia* had commenced her war duties as a troopship in 1941. By then she was already something of an old-timer as she had undertaken her maiden voyage as far back as 1913, when she was permanently placed on the Vancouver-Yokohama run. She was travelling with almost double her capacity of 1,238 in early February 1942, carrying reinforcements for the British garrison in Singapore, when she was attacked by five Japanese bombers 6 miles from her destination. Fire spread throughout the ship and she quickly became a floating inferno, drifting out of control. A number of survivors were rescued by the Australian sloop *Yarra*, but 16 men were lost. Ronald Thomas counted himself blessed. He had managed to swim clear of the ship and was picked up and brought safely to shore. Ten days later his luck changed entirely when he was captured as a Japanese prisoner of war. Somehow he still found the energy to keep up his war journal and, sweating in the intense heat and humidity of the jungle, he recorded how he made his escape from the *Empress of Asia*. I was therefore delighted when he gave me permission to include an extract from it here.

George Crow forced himself to return to Singapore in old age so that he could exorcise some of his personal demons. For him it was both necessary and cathartic. George died before we could meet, but when I spoke to his partner she gave me an extract from his private memoir, which he wrote to help him deal with the ghosts of his past. She said, 'George always told me that you have to live life to the full and not waste any opportunity. He would have wanted people to know about what happened. He wanted to people to understand so that all that suffering was important and meant something. Otherwise, what was it for?'

RONALD THOMAS

Written in Cell 44, Changi Jail, Singapore, 7th September 1945

❝ My twenty-first birthday on 4 February 1942 was a day of perfect weather, and rightly so for I was in the tropics. The sky was pure blue over which a scud of white cloud occasionally drifted. The sea remained one of green oil and the small undulations reflected the sun's glare with dazzling brilliance. From the ship's boat deck I could see, on either side, a strip of shimmering brown and green, which was land, but could discern no movement of any sort. Neither were there any buildings. It was as though every living thing slept in that stifling heat. Just ahead, and a little to the starboard side, the stern and the peculiar square funnels of the *Felix Lacelle* (our escort ship) were plainly visible. She was reputed to be carrying ammunition. The only change in that steadily moving line of ships was the escorting cruiser, which steamed up and down the convoy and was to be seen now to port and now to starboard. I stared with unseeing eyes at the land and tried to imagine what I would be doing if I were at home, but soon I ceased to daydream and left the rail.

Well, I thought, a twenty-first birthday needs some sort of celebration no matter where a fellow may be, so I made my way below to the crew canteen and purchased two cans of beer. (The beer sold in the troops' canteen was not fit to drink.) Clutching my precious cans I retraced my steps as far as my sleeping quarters, which were on the boarded-in weather deck. Here some fellows were writing or playing cards, a few were sleeping, but most of the occupants of the mess deck were enjoying the fresh air. I placed my beer in the rack above the mess table and decided to pay a visit to my old mate James 'Jock' Wallace before lunch. He was one of the several Bren-gun crews who were on duty on the raft deck and I liked to go up there because, for one thing, it was not crowded with troops but, more important still, they had an excellent pair of binoculars with which I studied the other ships and the silent coast.

I climbed the vertical ladder from A deck on to the concrete roof of a small cabin, which served as the gun platform, and greeted the gun crew. Jock's gun was on the starboard side, forward of the raft deck and alongside the forward funnel. I stayed there for about half an hour chatting, then decided to go below again. While climbing down I heard the drone of distant aircraft but took no particular notice as I thought they would probably be a force of British planes away on some mission. By the time I had reached the weather deck the drone of the planes was much louder and I could clearly see a formation of twenty-seven approaching the port side. Not giving it much thought I entered the mess deck to open one of my cans of beer and relax.

Just as I took one of the cans down the alarm bells rang. Everyone was instantly active. I left the beer unopened on the table and dived for my tin hat, a water bottle and iron ration, but I failed to find my lifejacket because someone else had taken it. By this time the mess deck was crowded and we were told to sit down at our respective places and await orders. Suddenly the harsh crackle of the machine-guns on the upper deck burst forth and we all flattened ourselves against the deck without waiting for orders. It was utterly silent. Then we heard a loud swish, which was instantly followed by a terrific explosion just outside our mess deck porthole, port side, and the air stank of explosive fumes. Paint and whitewash fell from the deck-head above in a fine cloud of dust. The guns up top still spat their defiance and a few more explosions occurred, but more distant now.

There was a clatter of footsteps down the companionway and an Army officer appeared. On entering the mess deck he told us that everything was under control but that he wanted volunteers to go down the stoke hold to keep the ship moving as some of the stokers had come up and refused to return. I came forward and was instructed that I would be required for the second shift.

Lunch was served (such as it was, because the food was filthy) and I rounded it off with a much-needed beer. After lunch I had occasion to go to the latrine – a filthy, stinking structure of wood and galvanised iron on the after part of the weather deck. While there I happened to remark to a fellow I knew that I had no lifejacket. He pointed to one hanging from a nail and said that it was there when he came in and as we were the only people in the place I might as well take it. I thank God that I did. The remainder of the day was uneventful and the feeling of tension eased somewhat as dinner-time approached. The vessel had suffered no direct hit but some lifeboats had been damaged by shrapnel.

The following day, 5 February, dawned like its predecessor but I, for one, had misgivings as to the end of it, although I comforted myself with the thought that if the Japs had really wanted to bomb us they would have sent another force in the afternoon of the previous day. By the way, only two or three planes detached themselves from the formation of twenty-seven, so I presumed that they had another target to go for. (The mystery was, where were *our* British fighters?)

I understand now that the officer in charge of the convoy expected another attack and therefore asked for the speed to be increased so that we could reach Singapore as soon as possible. Our ship, however, was the largest and oldest, and also, of course, the slowest, so the remainder of the convoy made all possible speed, leaving us to follow as fast as we could. Only the cruiser *Exeter* remained to protect us.

At approximately 10.45am the alarm bells jangled once more and once again we donned helmets, etc, and sat at the mess tables, only this time I had a lifejacket. We, of the volunteer stoker gang, had been told to wait until sent for. We waited. A deathly stillness had descended on the ship, and except for the pulsing of the engines nothing could be heard. A period like an age followed. Presently we heard the steady hum of approaching aircraft, which changed quickly from a hum to a furious roar. Instantly all hell was let loose. The stern gun shook the deck as it opened fire and the rattle and sound of the Bren and Bisa guns above was indescribable. Enemy bullets could be heard rattling against the funnels and metal plates of the top deck with savage ferocity.

There was an almighty crash. The ship trembled and vibrated from stem to stern as the first bomb found its target and we were all on the deck once more. Some chaps were under the wooden mess tables hoping they were bombproof. I was among them. I looked up and studied the faces around me. Everyone looked rather calm and, except for one fellow who was praying, no one seemed perturbed. The face of Captain Hill, our Group Officer, was dead white and his lips appeared strangely red in contrast to his bloodless cheeks.

Another crash! A bang! More hits were registered and dust flew everywhere. Meanwhile, the guns mounted on the ship rattled and thundered, letting go all they had. A squad of troops dashed by carrying a box of shell dressings for the wounded. A very white-faced and shaken QMS Kennedy arrived with the news that the first bombs had struck the vessel amidships and, piercing the upper decks, had entered the officers' lounge, causing terrific damage when they exploded. Kennedy's arms and legs were completely stripped of skin and he was trembling uncontrollably. Someone passed him a glass of water. Captain Lambert, our Regimental Officer, happened to be on the deck at the time and he asked Kennedy how things were. 'Pretty grim,' he replied coldly.

Meanwhile, the racket outside continued and more bombs stuck home. Approximately three-quarters of an hour had elapsed since the alarm bells had sounded. Where were the Hawkers and Hurricanes? An order was given to abandon ship. Captain Hill told us to proceed in an orderly manner to our lifeboat stations. It was then that I noticed one chap crying.

I grabbed my small haversack and made for the narrow companionway that led from our deck to the boat deck. We could only go up this way two at a time and even then one fellow had to be slightly in advance of the other. Our lifeboat station was situated near the centre of B deck, port side, but when we arrived there we found that to go forward to our station was impossible because the units whose stations were more forward that ours were already being driven back by the fierce flames that were surging sternwards. What with the pressure of troops returning aft and the force of the troops pushing up from below, something had to give. I found myself pinioned in a mass of men, unable to move my arms. So I dropped my haversack containing my camera and films, etc, and when I felt it underneath my feet, for some unaccountable reason I stamped on it. Next,

I found myself being propelled to the rail. I made up my mind to go over at the first opportunity. It was at this moment that I nearly trampled on a Major who was lying wounded on the deck. Strangely, I didn't feel any real fear, only a helpless annoyance that I found difficult to analyse.

I was forced towards the ship's rail and I wasn't sorry because the fire now had taken a strong hold and the ammunition in the cabins began to explode like firecrackers on Guy Fawkes Night. On nearing the rail I found myself opposite a lifeboat all ready to be lowered. I also perceived a short length or rope hanging from the deck above. I jumped for this and, catching it, heaved myself over the rail and into the almost empty lifeboat. I sat on the thwart, nearest the ship's side and facing forward. I can remember distinctly the white but outwardly calm face of Major Bowering (our CO) who was leaning on the rail smoking a cigarette as though on a pleasure cruise; the miserable look on Private Jones's face, who was standing next to him; and a line of dots astern, which I realised were the stokers who had already jumped overboard and were bobbing about in the sea.

More troops scrambled into the lifeboat until it was overloaded. Large lumps of burning paint were falling on my helmet, where they broke, sending a fiery cascade over my arms and legs. I knocked the stuff off quickly and luckily received no burns. One merchant seaman stood in the lifeboat and tried to lower it without success. He bawled to someone above to 'Lower away!', but we simply hung there for what seemed like ages before anything happened. Suddenly the forward end of the boat dropped with a sickening jerk while the stern remained fixed. This threw all the troops into a tangled struggling heap and one fellow, who was trapped beneath, began to shout and then screamed out in agony. But few heard him above the general din of gunfire, exploding ammunition and the roar of the now fiercely burning superstructure. My mate Jack Partridge and I yelled with all the power we possessed at the soldiers to get back – but we made no impression. Paddy Carberry's legs were trapped against a thwart and he was appealing with us to do something as he was clearly in terrible pain. The weight of the troops behind us was enormous – an almighty crushing force. I yelled again and then began to swear and curse at the mass of khaki in front of me until my throat hurt. However, the few who heard me were powerless to move because of the relentless pressure from behind them.

At that moment the aft pulley came free and we plummeted downwards, striking the sea with a resounding thwack. The lifeboat immediately began to fill with water through the holes where the drainage bungs should have been. For some reason, too, the lowering tackle could not be unhitched to release the boat. We desperately needed an axe to sever the fall ropes.

The *Asia* was still making a fair amount of speed and we were dragged through the sea at quite a pace. This didn't last long because the lifeboat began to rise up and I realised that she was about to capsize. Clutching the side of the boat I planted both fee on the thwart and waited in a crouching position until she had risen to something approaching 45 degrees. Then I struck out like a madman and experienced my one and only fear, for I dreaded the thoughts of the lifeboat crashing into my head. Actually, I must have been well clear in the first leap, but I didn't cease my frantic strokes until I was drained of all energy. On looking behind me I found that I was some distance now from the *Asia*, but I had visions of her exploding so I headed further away still.

After a few more strokes I turned once more and drank in the terrible scene before me. The *Asia* was now a mass of flames and smoke. This had driven the remaining troops to the stern, where the majority escaped by jumping on to the deck of the Australian sloop *Yarra*, which ran alongside for that purpose. She had come from Singapore. Suddenly the *Asia* began to swing around to port and I thought she would strike Horsburgh Light. Instead, she ran on into the sand banks where she stuck. Apparently the Captain ran her aground for safety.

By this time the sea was littered with troops, rafts, oars and wreckage of all descriptions. All this time I had been swimming aimlessly about from one piece of flotsam to the next until eventually I found a platform of wood that served as a raft and on which I rested. For some reason I had been singing 'I'm Twenty One Today' as loudly as I could from the time I got clear of the lifeboat, and many of the boys I knew shouted and waved to me, cheering me on.

Eventually a power launch spotted me and I was heaved aboard. Sitting down in the cabin I regained my breath. My chin was raw where it had rubbed against the rough fabric of the lifejacket. Later I was taken on board the *Yarra* where I was given hot sweet tea and some food, and was pleased to share some macaroni pudding with my old comrade Jock. Wrapped in a white blanket with my wet shirt and shorts in my arms, I made my landing on the island fortress of Singapore.

I considered the first day of my twenty-second year well begun!

GEORGE CROW

❝ It was defiance that made me go back to Singapore a few years ago. I wanted to show the world, 'Hey, look! I made it!' There were times out there during the war when I really didn't think I would, you see. In a way the *Empress of Asia* was just the start of a nightmare, just the beginning.

Our unit embarked on her on 25 January 1942. We had no idea where we were going, but the general consensus was that we were heading for the island fortress of Singapore to help out there.

The medical corps on board had no training on small arms, so my job was to train them up to be able to defend themselves and their patients. For the rest of the time I was manning guns on deck. On 1 February we were off the coast of Java. Suddenly we were bombed by the Japanese, but luckily they missed us! The ship was manned by Irish stokers from Liverpool who had opted for the Merchant Navy as opposed to the Army. They were a rough lot, but after the first attack they came up from the stoke hole and refused to go back down. Fortunately we had some ex-miners from Durham on board who went back down and stoked the ship.

However, by that time we had lost steam and this put us behind schedule. Thus, instead of arriving in Singapore in the dark we found ourselves in the Straits of Singapore at 11am in broad daylight. It was then that the real attack came. Japanese bombers came at us and one of the first bombs they dropped went into the midships area right down to the galley so that it was impossible to get from one end of the ship to the other. All the lifeboats were soon destroyed. We were ordered to abandon ship and make our way to the nearest life raft if we could. At this point we were about five miles from the shore in shark-infested water and a strong tide. Luckily for us an Australian sloop called the *Yarra* came alongside and took off a number of survivors, including me. All in all the raid had lasted about an hour.

The attack was frightening, but what came next was truly horrific. I was taken prisoner in Singapore and ended up working on the Deayn Railway on the Burma Road. You cannot imagine the depravation and torture we suffered. For over three years we barely had enough to eat and what with the heat and sickness we became the living dead. There is simply nothing I can compare it to and no way for me to describe the full horror of it. It was a living hell.

The nightmares of that time are still with me today. After the war I was able to put it to one side for a time, but it never truly leaves you. The cruelty of man is something extraordinary. However, I have returned to Singapore twice for reunions, which helps a little. They've actually built a hotel on the prison camp where I was all those years back. Unbelievable. I've been taken out to where the *Empress of Asia* ended her days and it brings it all back. But sometimes you have to revisit the past so that you can get on with the present, don't you?

Titanic threads...
Frances Partridge

Have been clearing out my cupboards to find some letters that Frances Partridge wrote to me a few years ago. I've been reading her war diary – *A Pacifist's War* – which is both absorbing and amusing. But where were those letters? I knew I had put them somewhere safe...

As a junior member of the fabled Bloomsbury Group, Frances Partridge knew well the likes of writers Virginia Woolf, Lytton Strachey and artists Vanessa Bell, Duncan Grant and Carrington. In fact, it was my love of Virginia Woolf's work that first brought me into contact with Frances in the first place.

Three years ago, after reading an article about the then 99-year-old Frances, I wrote to her asking her what Virginia Woolf was really like. She rang me up soon after and invited me for afternoon tea. So, on a boiling hot day in July 1999, we sat at a floridly painted table (executed by Duncan Grant) and sipped Earl Grey while she told me all about Virginia Woolf and the 'Bloomsberries'. Frances had bought a Cadbury's chocolate log and we did our best with that, despite the heat turning it into a syrupy gloop.

Like so many people of her age, Frances remembered the day she heard the news of the *Titanic* disaster. 'Oh yes, extremely well. There was such a lot of fuss, naturally – messenger boys shouting it out and all that. Everyone was in shock, you see.' Virginia Woolf had thought about writing a book about it and attended the British enquiry that followed the tragedy. In the event she didn't write the book, but she did write to her friend Ka Cox in apprehensive wonderment: 'Do you know it's a fact that ships don't sink at that depth, but remain poised halfway down and become perfectly flat, so that Mrs Stead is now like a pancake, and her eyes like copper coins.' (Mrs Stead was not actually on board, but her husband died that night.)

Frances told me that by far the most important thing she learned from the Bloomsbury Group was deep and lasting friendship. 'I've always been fortunate to have good and true friends. It's the one thing that has made life worth living.'

And the letters she wrote to me? They were tucked away in a box marked 'In case of Fire – SAVE THESE!'

ATHENIA
(1939)

12 March 2003

A letter today from Trevor Griffiths, whose sister Ceinwen Preddy survived the *Athenia* when it was torpedoed and sunk on 3 September 1939. It was sad news. Mrs Preddy had passed away at the grand old age of 98.

Mrs Preddy was more than happy to contribute her memories of the *Athenia* to my collection when I first wrote to her in 2000, and we had been trying to meet up ever since that time. She was in poor health on and off and somehow we could never find a suitable date to agree on. However, Mr Griffiths has been most thoughtful and furnished me with an voluminous scrapbook about the disaster, which includes all kinds of information about it – much of it personal. Enclosed was a letter dated 1939 that Mrs Preddy wrote to her aunt shortly after she was rescued, and a newspaper report in which she relives the horror and panic of it all for a reporter.

The Second World War was only a few hours old when the British Anchor Donaldson liner *Athenia*, bound from Liverpool to Montreal, was torpedoed and sunk 200 miles west of the Hebrides. Innocent civilians had been killed or endangered – including a substantial contingent of Americans who, as yet, had nothing to do with the war. Anyone who could remember the sinking of the *Lusitania* 28 years before must have wondered whether it was a grim case of history repeating itself.

Ceinwen Preddy (Gwen to family and friends) had boarded the ship at Liverpool. A few years previously she had emigrated to Canada from her native Wales and had subsequently got married there. Having had a relaxing holiday with her family she was eager to get back. Thus it was simply a case of bad timing when she found herself at sea at the start of the war. There were 1,103 passengers on board the *Athenia* – 75% of them women and children – who were trying to beat the clock in order to get across the Atlantic before the 'real' war started. Unluckily, U-30 was on patrol at the time and at 7.30pm its crew launched an attack. The *Athenia*'s wireless room was blown to bits and therefore an SOS could not be fired off into the night. Listing badly and sinking stern-first, it was difficult to launch the lifeboats and this accounted for many of the 112 lives lost. Rescue eventually came when two British destroyers, *Electra* and *Escort*, and an American freighter, *City of Flint*, arrived on the scene.

Strangely, the German authorities denied responsibility for the incident and U-30's commander Fritz-Julius Lemp was never court-martialled for his actions, claiming that he thought the *Athenia* was a British troopship. Less than a year later, Lemp was killed when his submarine U-110 was captured by the British Navy in the Baltic Sea. Stranger still, discovered on board the sub was an Enigma encoding machine, which enabled the Allied powers to track German U-boat traffic. Lemp, having fired the first shots of the Battle of the Atlantic, had thus unwittingly helped to finish it.

CEINWEN PREDDY

Canadian Pacific Telegraphs
Sep 5 1939 8.25am
SAFE GLASGOW DONT WORRY GOING HOME GWEN

22 September, 1939

Dear Margaret

A few lines hoping you are all well. Everyone fine here, though a bit worried at times, especially as six of the boys are of military age, but as yet none have been called up. We live in hopes. I wonder if you heard of my experience? I am fortunate to be here today, I think, as I was on the *Athenia* when she was torpedoed.

I was sailing home from Liverpool on 2 September, having been transferred from the *Aucania* (which was to have sailed from Southampton and on which I had booked my return passage). That ship was cancelled owing to the crisis. Little did I know what was in store for me.

We left Liverpool on the Saturday afternoon and it was 7.45pm on Sunday night when she was struck. I was seasick and in bed, but I knew immediately what had happened. There was a terrific noise and the lights went out (the portholes had all been closed down early in the afternoon). I jumped out of bed, grabbed my lifebelt and put it on. I had a thick dressing-gown on over my nightdress but nothing on my feet.

I managed to get up on to the deck, how I don't know, as there were women and children everywhere and a lot of wreckage on the stairway. I remained calm and wasn't at all frightened. Many lifeboats were filled and away before I had a chance to get into one. Fortunately it was still daylight and the ship didn't sink very fast.

I was in a lifeboat for eleven and a half hours. I shivered all night. It was biting cold and me with so little on. About four in the morning a destroyer was sighted. I was too seasick to look. We kept burning flares off and on all night, hoping and praying that we would be seen. It was around 9am Monday morning when the destroyer came alongside of us. I was an awful-looking sight by that time. There was water in the boat up to my knees with a lot of oil floating on it. I still had the lifebelt around my neck. Anyway, it was a grand feeling to be lifted on board that destroyer by two sailors!

I was wrapped in blankets and lifted into a bed. I think I slept most of the day. Tuesday morning at 11.30am we docked at Greenock, Scotland. There were cars waiting with clothes for us. After I had been fixed up with a dress, coat and shoes and stockings (along with everyone else) we were taken in buses – the ten of us – to three different hotels in Glasgow, about two and a half hours' journey from Greenock. I was at the Beresford Hotel there for two days, then was given my train fare to return home. As soon as we arrived I sent a cable home (also one to Canada). People were most kind to us everywhere and especially on that destroyer. You can imagine how I was welcomed home here. They had almost gone crazy here for they had happened to turn on the radio Monday morning at 8am and the first thing they heard was, 'The liner *Athenia*, which left Liverpool yesterday, has been torpedoed and is sinking fast.' It was an awful sensation for them all, as well as the folks in Toronto.

It was a sixteen-and-a-half-hour train journey from Glasgow, but I was so glad to get home. I was given the option of staying at the hotel along with many others until they could arrange another ship to take us back to Canada, but I couldn't face it straight away.

I have been home here now just two weeks and am expecting a wire any day now telling me to go back to Glasgow. Things are kept pretty secret about the sailing, but it is definite; we shall be convoyed next time. Of course, they don't like the thoughts of me attempting it again, but I should be very unhappy if I stayed here. I can't get back to my own home and husband quick enough now. It will probably be a dreadful trip but <u>I'm game</u>!

Well dear, I hope I haven't bored you with my tale and I'm hoping by the time you read this that I'll be on or near Canadian soil again. There's nothing like it now.

Love to you all,

Ceinwen xxxx

11 HOURS IN OPEN BOAT

JORDANSTON WOMAN'S ORDEAL

'A NIGHTMARE EXPERIENCE'

Mrs G. Preddy, eldest daughter of Mr and Mrs T. Griffiths, of Trecoed, Jordanston, who was on the sunken liner *Athenia*, as mentioned in our last issue, arrived home on Saturday from Glasgow.

Mrs Preddy spent 11 hours in an open boat clad only in her night clothing and a bath robe.

'It was a nightmare experience,' she said to a representative.

Speaking of tension among the ship's passengers on the fateful Saturday, she said, 'Some had been wondering if we were safe, and I personally had assured two ladies that everything was all right.

'I was in bed when it happened, as I had not been well. Immediately the lights went out. I managed to find my lifebelt, which had been placed at the foot of the bed, and, wrapping a bath robe around me, I went on deck. After about 15 minutes I was placed in a lifeboat, which was more fortunate than some of the others. We were in it nearly 11 hours before a destroyer picked us up.

NO PANIC

'Nobody seemed to talk very much. We saw destroyers arrive on the scene but they did not seem to come our way and we sent up flares. It was not until almost nine o'clock the following morning that we were picked up. Our boat had been stationary all the time as a sea anchor had been dropped. I was nursing a young child at one end of the boat and its mother at the other end, with another child, kept crying out, "Are you all right, John?"

Mrs Preddy said there was no panic. With other survivors she was landed at Greenock on Tuesday morning. She paid high tribute to the officers and men of the destroyer which picked her up.

'They did everything possible for us and made us very comfortable.'

At Greenock the survivors were given clothes and coats and were taken by bus to hotels at Glasgow.

One of Mrs Preddy's most vivid memories is that of the breaking away of a lifeboat in which a number of children had been placed first.

'They managed to save some of them,' she added, sadly.

Titanic threads...
Harry Slight

'In Southampton, good old sea port
Wives made widows, what a list;
But so recently together
Husbands now forever missed.'
Edwin Drew

When the news of the *Titanic* disaster reached Southampton it seemed as if the populace had been hit by a biblical plague – 549 local crew members had been lost. In such a close-knit seafaring community the effect was devastating. Eye witnesses of the day reported that a preternatural silence descended on the area such as no other in living memory. Southampton was a city besieged by mourning.

'Flags flew at half mast in the city, and in the districts of Northam and Shirley, where nearly every man made his living from the sea, there were many stricken homes. Every one of the modest brick cottages in Russel Street contained a sorrowing family.'
Titanic and Silent Cinema, Steven Bottomore

Even today it is said that many local people in Southampton still have a direct family connection with the disaster. I recently had the opportunity to talk to a native Sotonian, whose grandfather served as a member of the crew on board the *Titanic*. I suspect that her story is one that would find a similar counterpart in many a family within a five-mile radius of the *Titanic*'s home port.

'The *Titanic* story was a part of our family. I grew up with it. My mother, grandmother and I lived together in Southampton, because my father had been drowned at the seaside, so we were very close. In fact, my grandmother would mention the *Titanic* often enough for it to become almost commonplace. I never gave it much thought at the time – it was just there, always in our lives.
My grandfather, Harry John Slight, was killed on the *Titanic*. He was

87

a third class steward and only 34 years old. His body was never recovered. He had married my grandmother, Agnes, in 1902 and together they had three children: my mother Jessie, Harry, and the baby of the family, Winifred. My grandfather had signed on to the Royal Marines when he was 18 and had acted as a personal steward. After leaving there with excellent references he looked for work on the liners. By all accounts he was proud to be taken on by the White Star Line and was optimistic that it would all work out fine and he would be able to support his little family with a regular income of £3 15s per week.'

Sailing day was a particularly busy time for stewards like Harry Slight. The *Titanic*'s third class passengers began boarding at Southampton between 9.30 and 11.00am:

'Hurried along by stewards' gestures and urgings, they descended the steel stairways and entered the maze of corridors along which their small cabins were located. There seemed to be no regularity to the cabins' numbering and there were frequent pauses, questions, discussions with stewards (often accompanied by raised voices) and emphatic gestures. Up and down the veitchi-floored, steel-walled corridors the voices sounded, bringing the first presence of passengers to the ship's lower reaches: the shrill cries of children, the angry misunderstandings of adults, the confused murmurs and the subdued rush of third class passengers aboard *Titanic*.'

Titanic: Triumph and Tragedy, Eaton and Haas

But at Queenstown things were a little calmer:

'There was less hectic activity than there had been at Southampton... The stewards and attendants knew the ship's layout and their duties better than they had before; they, too, were in the process of "shaking down" just as the ship was. And the passengers were more tractable too: "At least this lot spoke English," one said.'

Eaton and Haas

My correspondent continued:

'My mother told me about the day the news of the *Titanic* sinking reached Southampton. She was eight years old at the time and was in a local shop when she overheard some of the customers talking about it. Imagine the shock! After all, she knew her father was on board and she didn't know if he'd be coming back. She hurried home because she didn't know what to make of it. Was it true? However, when she got home there were neighbours standing outside staring at the house and the terrible realisation dawned on her. Their silent vigil spoke volumes. In fact, it was little Jessie who had to break it to my grandmother.

Naturally she was heartbroken and totally grief-stricken. There were many tears shed in that house during the days that followed. Harry and Agnes had only been married ten years and had been extremely happy together. I remember her telling me how she and Harry loved going to the music hall to see Marie Lloyd. It was a simple life but a contented one. The *Titanic* tore her life apart for a while.

Fortunately the Titanic Relief Fund stepped in to help. Agnes was awarded £288 outright for Harry's death, then smaller regular payments to assist with raising her three children. When I was a child, a Miss Newman, who was the 'Titanic Lady Visitor', used to call on my grandmother. She lived in Hawthorn Cottage on the Common in Southampton. I think she was the daughter of the house and she appeared to me to be very upper class. Remember, there was quite a class barrier back then. The relief fund allowed my mother to leave school at the age of thirteen (a year early) and attend a secretarial course at De Bears' Secretarial School in Southampton. Winifred also did a similar course at the Gregg School, while Harry was apprenticed to a local upholsterer by the name of Pascoe. All in all the three children were given a good start in life as a result of the relief fund.

Before starting at the De Bears' Secretarial School my mother was taken by someone connected with the fund to buy a new outfit and it was suggested that she should have brown as it would 'suit her colouring'. When she attended the school she found that *all* the "Titanic girls" were dressed in brown, except for one who had refused to wear it. (Her mother had died and her sister persuaded her to go for blue instead!) The "non Titanic girls" dressed in clothes of their own choice. Can you imagine that? The disaster even colour-coded the poor.

My grandmother didn't mind discussing the disaster but she got very upset when the film *A Night to Remember* was released in the 1950s. I can remember that well because she said it should never have been made – she felt it was too soon after the disaster. There were still so many local people alive who had painful memories of it. The *Titanic* was so personal to her and the idea of a film just brought the heartache of losing Harry rushing back.

Life had to go on, however, and in 1913 Agnes remarried. Don't forget she had three children to bring up single-handed, which must have been a lonely and exhausting task. She had another son, my Uncle Stanley, but incredibly the sea claimed him, too. He was killed when his submarine was attacked in 1941 during the Second World War. However, like so many women of her generation she was made of strong stuff and always kept her spirits up. In those days you just had to put your emotions to one side and tackle life head on. What else could she do? My grandmother never forgot Harry, though. She saved all his private papers, including his death certificate, and stored them safely away to the end of her life in 1960. You see, they were so very much in love and those feelings last for ever.'

LAKONIA
(1963)

1 June 2003

The story how the *Lakonia* caught fire and sank on 22 December 1963 made the headlines in both the national and regional press. When survivor Helen Gartside arrived home she was surprised to find a reporter from the local *Gazette* waiting for her. Her story appeared on the front page in the next edition, where readers could wonder at the brave woman's ordeal. She told me all about it herself when I spoke to her, and she sent me that front page to add to this collection. Equally fascinating is her statement from the official enquiry, which I've also pasted in below. 'It's all there dear,' she said, 'one way or another. A sad old tale, isn't it?'

Alice Julius felt emotionally scarred by the trauma of the entire event, and without any counselling on hand she decided to get it out of her system by writing it all down. Her daughter Susan, who, as a child of eight, was travelling with her parents, wondered if I would like to hear her memories of the trip, and both versions compliment each other accordingly.

Joyce Murrell contacted me by letter, and its tone perfectly encapsulates the feelings of worry and uncertainty that many a survivor must have felt the night the *Lakonia* went up in flames.

'Here is a holiday with all the risks removed!' boasted the Greeks Line's advertisement for sailings on its newly acquired *Lakonia* in 1963. And again: 'Here is a holiday you will remember and talk about for the rest of your life!' The promotional material was right. The *Lakonia*'s 'maiden voyage' certainly turned out to be memorable for everyone concerned – but for all the wrong reasons.

The *Lakonia* left Southampton on 19 December 1963 on an 11-day Christmas cruise around the Canary Islands. She was carrying 1,063 passengers and crew, who were looking forward to the more temperate climate of the Mediterranean. Two days later, on the night of the 'Tramps Ball', a small fire broke out in the hairdressing salon. It quickly took hold and spread because of the ship's outdated or ineffectual fire-fighting equipment. In circumstances eerily similar to the *Morro Castle* 30 years before, there were no official instructions given out to passengers and most of them had to fend for themselves. Because of a fatal breakdown in communication, 131 people were either drowned or left unaccounted for.

The *Lakonia* was not a new ship. The Greek Line purchased the 30-year-old liner *Johan Van Oldenbarnveldt* from the Nederland Royal Mail Line and had her refitted for the burgeoning cruise market in early 1963. Whether her refit had been a rush job is a moot point, because diverse opinions both praising and condemning the condition of the *Lakonia* appeared in print immediately after the disaster. One thing is clear: the lifeboats on board the *Lakonia* caused the crew problems from the start. Some could not be launched because of faulty mechanisms, while those that could had an alarming propensity to take on water. On the *Titanic* there simply weren't enough lifeboats; the *Lakonia*'s lifeboats had room for everyone, yet here is a depressingly familiar story of innocent lives being sacrificed. It appeared that in 1963 lessons that should have been learned about the necessity of well-planned lifeboat drills way back in 1912 had not been heeded. Here was history repeating itself with all its attendant calamities. Friday, January 3,1964

HELEN GARTSIDE

TEN HOURS OF UTTER PANIC AND FEAR

Local Woman Describes *Lakonia* Disaster

Safely back in Bovington recovering from a three-hour ordeal by sea following the *Lakonia* disaster, Mrs Helen Gartside this week retold her story of the tragedy.

At her Green Lane home, Mrs Gartside described to a *Gazette* reporter the ten hours of 'utter panic and fear' that ensued after fire broke out in the ill-fated Greek liner off Madeira last week.

Attractive Mrs Gartside, anticipating what had promised to be the Christmas of a lifetime, had gone to her cabin to write a few postcards. Then the fire broke out. 'I went down again to the lounge bar where we had been dancing beforehand. What I saw there shocked me,' she said. 'A handful of crew were drinking heavily straight from the bottle. They were all Greek and were shouting and laughing.

'There were certainly not enough fire-hoses available and some of the passengers were asked to try to fight the flames with buckets of water. They weren't even fire buckets.

ENORMOUS BANG

'We sat there and waited and I saw a crack appear in the ceiling. There was an enormous bang, which was the first explosion, but I was told that it was only the noise of deckchairs being thrown overboard.

'We all went up on deck and saw some of the lifeboats being lowered. The Greek crew were pushing and shoving and there was simply no order at all.'

Like hundreds of other passengers, Mrs Gartside found no room in a lifeboat and was left on the ship after all the boats had been lowered. The order for her to abandon ship was given by the Entertainments Officer at about 5am – six hours after the fire started and after three explosions had shaken the liner.

After being in the water for three hours, Mrs Gartside was picked up by the rescue ship *Montcalm* and hauled on deck by lifeline, there to be wrapped in warm blankets and put to bed in a crew cabin.

'WONDERFUL'

'The people aboard the *Montcalm* were absolutely wonderful,' said Mrs Gartside. 'They gave us brandy and hot coffee and all the crew went out of their way to help us. More blankets and cigarettes were dropped to us by aircraft and they really looked after us well, giving us clothes and food.'

After landing at London Airport during the afternoon of Christmas Day, Mrs Gartside had to call at a cleaner's to collect a coat and skirt – all she had, except the dress she was wearing, was left on board. Her gold watch was ruined by sea water. Luckily her possessions were insured.

Sadly, Mrs Gartside added, 'This has all been a terrible shock to me. I only hope that I shall forget the bad things soon and only remember the good points.'

Helen Gartside: Official Enquiry Transcript

My cabin was S.29 on the Sun Deck and at about 10.55pm I went up to my cabin to write some postcards. While I was writing I heard four bells ringing weakly. They did not appear to me to be fire bells so I continued with my employment and once again I heard the four bells. I thought it was someone impatiently ringing for a steward.

I then heard the footsteps of people rushing and it occurred to me that there must be something wrong. I opened my cabin door and the corridor was completely full of dense smoke. I grabbed my lifejacket and followed other passengers down the staircase. On reaching the promenade deck we were all told to go to the dining room. I sat there for about ten minutes and was then told to go upstairs again. I did so and saw people milling around the boat deck rails, and it seemed the lifeboats were to be lowered – which they were. We couldn't get to our lifeboat station – No 11 – because of the confusion, and I stood at the rail with two men and a lady and they said we must get into the lifeboat. By this time people were jumping into them, men, women and children. We could not get into this lifeboat so we waited for another. As my friend Mrs Hobras climbed the rail, someone shouted 'Full up!' and there seemed no more available. Mrs Hobras and I turned round and stepped back. But I saw there was difficulty in lowering this lifeboat too. I also noticed a crew member chopping at the rope, and when we turned round and walked towards the lounge somebody held me aside and said we were not to go out on to the boat deck again because that lifeboat had capsized.

We remained in the lounge until 5.30am the following morning. I was disgusted to see members of the crew drunk and some were making passes at me. I got so cross I said, 'You ought to be fighting the fire, not drinking,' but they just laughed. Some time during the night the Purser, Mr Bogetti, came and said we were safe for the next four or five hours as they had the fire under control, and from that moment on, so far as I was concerned, nobody seemed to worry about it.

My two companions, Mrs Hobras and Mr Elliott, went down to Mr Elliott's cabin to see if they get some of his belongings. They came up again and Mr Elliott said his cabin had been completely looted and Mrs Hobras said she went to the stokers and accused them of it. At this point I was sitting with my back to the windows on the port side of the Mocambo Lounge when I noticed a lot of thick, black smoke rising again a little way down the deck on the port side. Within a few minutes there were flames everywhere. (I think the time may have been 4.30am.) Somebody shouted out for volunteers and I noticed a dozen or so male passengers run through with small buckets. There had been two explosions up to this time and I left the Mocambo Lounge and made my way to the starboard side. There was no panic but a great deal of confusion. My friends and I stood on the starboard deck not knowing what to do – nobody up to this time had given any precise orders – in addition, the fire was getting much worse and coming out on to the starboard side of the deck.

I do not know who gave the order to move right up to the enclosed part of the stern, but not seeing any officer I suppose it must have been Mr Herbert, the Cruise Director. From his demeanour and the state of his clothing, you could tell that he had clearly been fighting the fire. I did not, however, see any other members of the crew doing anything about it. Somebody shouted to get the glass doors open and I helped other passengers pull these up and assisted two crew members (I believe they were Germans) to drop a tangled rope ladder over the side of the ship. When I went to Mr Herbert, not seeing anyone else to ask, and said, 'Shall we go overboard?' he said, 'Yes, you must go now.' Then he shouted an order: 'Ladies and gentlemen, the fire is becoming too great for us to remain on board – we must abandon ship.' With that, I got over the rail, kicked my shoes off and went down the rope ladder into the water. I think it was about 5.30 or 5.45am, although my watch had stopped by the time I was picked up. I just swam until eventually after about three hours I reached the *Montcalm* [a rescue ship] and was pulled up by lifeline.

I make no criticism of the crew during the launching of the lifeboats but only about the crew and their drinking. Generally, I do criticise the lack or organisation and I think the fire-fighting equipment was totally inadequate.

ALICE JULIUS AND HER DAUGHTER SUSAN PRIDAY

66 We arrived at Southampton on 19 December to find the *Lakonia* gaily decked out with flags. We were shown to our cabins, which were spotlessly clean, by a smiling steward and stewardess who gave the impression that they were happy to welcome us aboard. The whole ship had a happy holiday air. If you wished you could partake of the organised entertainments – or alternatively you could just sit and watch the sea go by.

At 10pm on the Sunday night, I was taking part in the carol service and when this had finished I joined my husband for a drink. We wandered off to a bar at the aft end of the ship and had just ordered our drinks when a woman passenger appeared and yelled out, 'Fire!' Quite frankly I thought maybe she was drunk, and together with other passengers at the bar we took little notice. It did occur to me that perhaps someone at the Tramps Ball had had the bright idea of lighting a fire in the ballroom – but apart from that I didn't give her a second thought. But when volumes of black smoke came rolling out of the public room we realised that something was very wrong. At this stage stewards appeared and opened the big windows on the promenade deck – presumably with the idea of letting out the smoke, but which in fact let in air, and as everyone knows, gusts of air are not conducive to putting out a fire.

My nine-year-old daughter Susan was asleep in her cabin and my husband and I set off to get her out. For some reason we split up and I met with some opposition from the stewards, who told be that it was impossible to get through. To those of you who have children, you can imagine that the word 'impossible' has no meaning when your child is in danger. Despite lots of smoke I made it – but I leave you to imagine my feelings when I found her cabin empty!

Susan: My first memories are of being awoken by two strange people. This was an unnerving experience for an eight-year-old. There was smoke, a strong smell of burning and the floor was very hot to stand on in bare feet. The couple that found me were very calm and the man carried me to an upper deck. Some men (crew?) were wearing gas masks, and to this day I am absolutely petrified of such masks, eg in war films and on display in museums. As I was shivering with cold, the man stood on a piano stool and tore down a curtain to wrap around me. Having had instilled in me 'right from wrong' at a very early age, I knew this was a terrible thing to do and was very pleased when I was rescued from this 'terrible' man by my mother.

Mrs Julius: With a very sick heart I made my way back to the promenade deck – not knowing what to do next – when I heard my name being called.

It was an elderly couple, who had made it their business to go along and knock on the cabin doors, warning passengers, and they brought Susan up with them. I have since wondered why the stewards had not roused those passengers who were asleep, but assume I shall never know the answer. I afterwards tried to contact these folk but failed to do so and don't know even if they were saved.

Susan, clad in pyjamas but wrapped around with a curtain that had been torn down from somewhere, sat down with me quietly waiting for my husband to find us. At this stage neither of us had lifejackets, but a steward opened a locker and handed some out. Previously we had found a lot of deck rugs and as most of the women were in light dresses these we found very acceptable. The steward tied the lifejacket around me (over the deck rug) and gave me the following instructions: 'If you have to go into the water, madam, untie your lifejacket, remove the rug and replace your lifejacket.' To a non-swimmer like me, this was disturbing advice! However, my husband rearranged the straps, and I was able to move freely.

There were a number of passengers milling around and without any panic we all drifted towards our lifeboat station. It was impossible to get to the exact spot as the so-called fire-fighting team were using that part of the deck – presumably in an effort to get to the source of the fire. Had it not been so tragic it would have been funny – the sort of set-up that would cause gales of laughter in a pantomime. One man with a fireman's helmet trooped past followed by one with a gas mask, one with a fire extinguisher and yet another with a wet cloth around his mouth. After all that it was discovered that the pumps were out of order!

Eventually we managed to get to our lifeboat station and once again we sat around on deckchairs wondering what the next step was to be. The Cruise Director, a Mr Herbert, then came along and said, 'The Captain has given orders for the boats to be lowered.' I guess it may sound extremely stupid, but I honestly believed that we were going out for a row on the sea until they had the fire under control and we would all return. I even got so far as to thinking how our clothes would smell of smoke when we got back. Thus we got into a lifeboat. Nobody appeared to be in charge and the passengers were not seated correctly and we could have taken at least as many again. It also seems odd to me that we had quite a number of crew in our boat, and in particular the Second Officer – which somehow seemed out of keeping with the British tradition of 'women and children first'.

Susan: My next memory is of being lowered into the lifeboat. I was with my father and although I knew my mother was in the same boat we had become separated. I remember seeing faces, presumably of trapped people, in the portholes, and my father burying my head in his chest. The lifeboat was tipping and heaving at a frightening angle and hitting the water with a terrific bang. After he was rescued, the ship's Padre sat next to us and prayed aloud for the entire time in the lifeboat, and the female passenger opposite me was extremely seasick. I slept standing up in between my father's legs. I remember so well being woken up by him saying, 'Sue, look at this – you will never see anything like this again in your life!' In between the huge waves I could see the ship ablaze from what seemed like bow to stern. Oddly the words 'LAKONIA' were still visible – brightly illuminated by light bulbs.

Mrs Julius: The lifeboat alongside us was then lowered – but something went wrong as the people in that boat were hurled into the water and I can still recall their terrified screams as they were pitched into the sea. Our lifeboat was then lowered, but again the mechanism jammed and we were hanging at a fearful angle for what seemed an eternity. We finally hit the sea with a mighty splash, crashing against the side of the ship. The next wave enabled us to get clear of the hull and we were away. The propeller on the lifeboat had been smashed and in the darkness we heard a call for help. With great difficulty we managed to locate the *Lakonia*'s resident Padre. It was only then, when I was able to look at the ship, that I realised just how big the fire was.

For hours the crew rowed magnificently, and at about 7am one of them told me that there was a rescue ship in the area and we would be safe. All I could see were mountains of water, but when we rode the waves we could discern a searchlight sweeping the sea. It kept sweeping past us and you have no idea what it feels like to be sitting absolutely helpless in a small boat willing a searchlight to catch you in its beam. Finally it found us and the crew rowed us towards the ship – the *Salta*. But our troubles were far from over.

There was a heavy swell running and the lifeboat crashed repeatedly against the side of the *Salta*'s hull. Willing and ready as the crew of the ship were to pick us up, they seemed to have little idea of what was the best method. If you have ever stood on a quay looking up at a liner, you will begin to have some idea of its immense height from sea level. It is like a steel wall. Firstly, they lowered the ship's companionway but the lifeboat crashed against this, splintered it and rendered it useless. Next, they dropped flexible ladders over, and whilst it was impossible for the elderly folk to get up these, the crew of the *Lakonia* managed it after securing our lifeboat to the *Salta*. As a consequence we passengers were left in the lifeboat supposedly to work things out for ourselves!

Eventually a member of the *Salta* climbed down and so began the operation of getting us on to the ship. This was done by means of a rope lowered from the promenade deck and fastened around the waist of each passenger, who was then individually hoisted up. My husband had managed to get aboard, but Sue and I sat in the lifeboat watching the other passengers. Then our turn came. Susan looked rather like an angel as she floated upwards, still clad in her pyjamas. I have no clear recollection of being rescued because, having seen Sue up safely, I fainted.

Susan: After rowing clear of the *Lakonia* I remember the searchlight from the rescue ship scouring the mountainous waves for us and the cheer when we were finally located. I was very frightened when we were up close against the *Salta*. My father jumped from the lifeboat and only just managed to grab hold of the broken gangway in an endeavour to explain to the crew that it was impossible for some of the passengers to leave the lifeboat and attempted to suggest other methods of evacuation to them. A member of the crew was lowered down the side of the *Salta* on a rope and made a bee-line for me, which was a little unsettling. I assume this was in an attempt to rescue the children first. I actually recall the journey up the side of the *Salta* on a rope as being great fun!

Mrs Julius: As I awoke I was conscious of being surrounded by people. Someone was trying to get rum down my throat, though this was a bit difficult as I was in a bad state of shock and trembling violently. Another person was inspecting me to see if I needed any first aid, and a doctor was standing by with a hypodermic syringe. After being given a shot I was half led, half carried to a cabin and a kindly stewardess endeavoured to remove my dress without undoing the zip.

The *Salta* was a bit grim when compared to the relative luxury of the *Lakonia*. It was an emigrant ship, en route for South America. We wryly hoped she was fireproof. Still, it seemed like heaven after our ordeal in the lifeboat. Under maritime law, rescue ships stand by for twelve hours from the time they pick up the first survivor, and for the next few hours we lined the decks watching for boats. Unfortunately we also witnessed a large number of dead bodies which came drifting by.

Finally we made it to Madeira on Tuesday morning. Sue had been fitted out in some clothes that had been found for her on the *Salta*. I was still in a very oil-splashed frock and with only one shoe. My possessions at that time consisted of my reading glasses and a tattered carol sheet, which somehow I had clutched throughout the whole sorry affair.

The people of Funchal were absolutely stunned by the whole thing. They lined the streets of the town as the coaches containing the survivors made their way to the hotel in which we had previously stayed in happier circumstances. We were allocated to various hotels and in due course given what was considered the essential items of clothing and after a rather dreary week we came back to England.

Susan: On arrival in Madeira I remember being taken by coach somewhere and the street was lined with local people. My mother was most insistent that we were to wave enthusiastically to show everybody that we were OK.

Mrs Julius: The kindness that was bestowed on Sue and I was so very touching. There was the maid in the hotel who gave me her cardigan, the flower-seller who gave us some money to buy coffee, and so many other small gestures One well-known resident of Funchal stopped Sue and I in the street and said, '*Lakonia*?' and on being told, 'Yes,' took his scarf from his neck and wrapped it around Sue. This was my undoing – I wept. It later transpired that he followed us to our hotel and in very broken English and with the assistance of the maid, made us understand that he would call for us and would we have tea in his house? When we arrived we found that the family had decked out a Christmas tree with presents especially for Sue. These we shall always treasure and all the memories of those dear people.

Susan: We returned to England on the *Transvaal Castle* as my father wouldn't fly. During a game of board bingo I slipped while retrieving a ticket and sustained a black eye. My mother was incredulous that we had all survived such a terrible tragedy and yet I was to return to Southampton to be met by many relatives looking dramatically injured with a black eye received from simply slipping on a polished floor!

It's odd how the *Lakonia* has been forgotten. People talk about the *Titanic* as if it were the only ship that ever sank! But the *Lakonia* was an awful disaster really, and just as bad in many ways.

Mrs Julius: Word did not reach home of our safe rescue for some time. Although the news of the disaster broke in England on the Monday morning, it wasn't until early on Wednesday morning that our relatives received cablegrams with news. More drama followed when somehow Sue was posted as 'Missing possibly in Casablanca', so there was much relief when we all arrived safely in Southampton on Friday 3 January. It was only at that moment that our loved ones knew for sure that all three of us had come safely through our ghastly experience.

JOYCE MURRELL

❝ We had decided to take a cruise as a holiday that winter as this would be something new and interesting. My husband and I were in the hotel trade and we felt we were due a break. We planned to stop off at Las Palmas and rejoin the ship on its next round trip. On this cruise we only needed to get the children excused from school for two days at the end of term. Our eldest boy, Dennis, was thirteen and a half and due to start at boarding school in January. Ironically, my husband had had a heart attack and we felt this would be restful.

On the night of the 22nd the two boys, my husband and myself were watching a Bob Hope film, *Call Me Bwana*, which kept breaking down between reels. Consequently we were still up when we were told about the fire. A good thing, too, because it was in the area of the boys' cabins and we couldn't get to them. My daughter Christine was at the Tramps Ball wearing jeans and her father's shirt, but my husband was able to get to our cabin and collect coats.

It was a very frightening time from then on, particularly when we got to our lifeboat station. Someone came along and said, 'I think women and children first, gentlemen,' and the children and I were given a lifejacket and put into a boat. The other passengers in it were anxious to get away from the ship in case we were pulled under it. There was plenty of frantic but chaotic rowing until my daughter – who had rowing experience – got the men organised. She took charge of our youngest son, Laurence, and I hung on to Dennis as he was hanging over the side with bad seasickness. I sat there still picturing my husband left alone on the deck (something I shall never forget). A man in the lifeboat with his wife and son tried to tell me I was 'All right now', which didn't go down very well. Later, someone who had a torch was signalling SOS, which for some reason seemed rather amusing at the time. Eventually we were rescued by a ship called the *Salta*. We climbed up a rope ladder, had our lifejackets cut off (they were apparently obsolete), given some brandy and settled on board. We slept in bunk beds right down in the bowels of the ship, which was not terribly good for the nerves.

It was then on to Madeira and up to Funchal. The guest house we were taken to had not expected to operate for another week and had to have a cooker rushed in. We were all feeling upset and when we heard a rescue ship was coming in, my daughter and another girl rushed down to the dock to see if there was any news. They came back with a suitcase each and clothing. A big store had opened to provide basic supplies. This was some comfort as all we had were the clothes we left the ship in. We counted ourselves lucky that we hadn't been in our nightclothes like so many others.

But where was my husband, the man of the house? That was the only question for us. We were so terribly upset not to know what had become of him. On Christmas morning, when we went to the shipping office, a gentleman called out, 'Your husband is safe! He's been taken to Casablanca.' We stood with our arms around each other and cried and cried with relief.

Later we decided to come home on the *Lakonia*'s sister ship, *Arkadia*. Some people insisted on waiting to fly home, but it was quicker this way. The first night on board I couldn't go to bed but we gradually relaxed and we had a much calmer crossing home. Pretty soon the welcome sight of Plymouth Sound hove into view. It was a beautiful sunny day and our hopes were high. We had to stop at one point to take on board a team of people to make enquiries about the disaster.

To see my husband come on board to greet us was the best part of the journey home, and the best Christmas present for us all. We were just so pleased to be all together again. My husband and I took the children to London for a few days to see some shows and give them happier memories of their holiday. But we were all so affected by the experience, it was at least a year before we were really able to talk about it. However, my husband told me later what had happened to him.

When he went down to the cabin he found that our cameras, jewels and money had disappeared and Christmas presents were unwrapped. After abandoning ship he was in the sea for six hours, but a wooden deckchair floated near and he was able to cling to that. The fact that the water was relatively warm also made a huge difference. We were all so glad to be alive that other things did not seem important. Life simply took on a sharper perspective for the five of us.

Titanic threads...
Sidney Sedunary

The Christmas holidays. A card from Sidney Sedunary this morning. It's always a pleasure to receive any communications from Sid and I shall add it to my growing collection of correspondence from him. I've known him for a few years now and he's a real *Titanic* enthusiast himself with an ever-growing collection of scrapbooks about the subject. He's also a gentleman and a dear friend.

I first met him in July 2000 when he invited me over to talk about his father, also Sidney, who was a steward on the *Titanic*. There were plenty of things I wanted to ask him and he didn't hesitate to help. There was no patter either – he really thought about each point he made, which was both considerate and refreshing.

The events leading up to and including the actual disaster are endlessly fascinating, there's no doubt about that. However, I'm always interested in the postscript: what was it like for those left behind and how did they cope? Sid's father was killed on the *Titanic*. His body was later identified and buried at sea. I will never forget the moment when Sid handed me the wedding ring his father had been wearing on the night the *Titanic* went down, or indeed his father's smoking pipe, which was found in his pocket. It was a humbling experience and a treasured memory for my lifetime. Sid was also kind enough to let me record his story.

'My father was very happy to be going on the *Titanic*. Just before he signed on as assistant to the Third Class Chief Steward, he had been serving on the *Olympic* (the *Titanic*'s sister ship), which, strangely enough, had a reputation for being an unlucky ship. In her few months of service she had had a number of mishaps – the most notorious being a collision with HMS *Hawke* in the Solent. My father was told that he would be taken off the *Olympic* to serve on the *Titanic* while the *Olympic* was being repaired in Belfast.

I have a letter written by my father to my mother dated 27 January 1912, which explains some of his anxieties about the 'unlucky' *Olympic*:

"I expect we shall be late getting in as we have lost a blade of the propeller and so we have been going a lot slower. My word! What do you say, this is a lucky ship, eh? Always something the matter... We are waiting back this time for the *Titanic* so, Dearie, we shall have a little longer together."

My father came home to Southampton to spend some time with my mother before joining the *Titanic*, and that is when I was conceived. I have no idea if my father knew for sure that my mother was pregnant before he left, although my mother maintained that he did.

My parents had been married on 15 October 1911, only six months before the disaster. My mother had been born on 15 July 1890, so when the ship sank on 15 April 1912 she had an aversion to that number and was worried I would be born on the 15th – but I broke the cycle. Luckily I arrived a bit earlier on 4 December 1912.

Years later my mother told me that before the *Titanic* had sailed she had been suspicious about the ship's 'unsinkable' reputation, but apparently my father was fully confident in the safety of the vessel, as were other members of the crew. It's ironic when you consider that the *Titanic* sank on her very first trip, and the 'unlucky' *Olympic* wasn't retired from service until 1935.

My father had joined the Royal Navy at the age of seventeen in 1904 and had served on a number of ships until he commenced work with the White Star Line on the *Adriatic* and later the *Olympic*. He was the oldest of seven children, born in Newbury, Berkshire, in March 1887. (We sometimes forget that it was common to have large families in those days.) Both he and my mother were only in their twenties when they married and came to live in Southampton. For a while he tried working on shore, but pretty soon he went back to sea. My mother must have been devastated by his death, and with no state benefits it can't have been any fun finding you were pregnant with no means of support.

However, after the disaster my mother was fortunate enough to receive thirteen shillings a week from the Titanic Relief Fund for my schooling. I can remember a very austere-looking lady called Miss Newman who used to come round with money every month. We received that until I was sixteen. My mother also told me that shortly after the disaster she was visited by the Mayoress of Southampton, who pressed a gold sovereign into her hand.

We didn't stay long in Southampton and eventually moved to Reading. My mother, who up until that time had never met my father's family, fell in love with my father's younger brother Arthur. They couldn't marry straight away because at the time it was illegal to wed your deceased husband's brother, but after the First World War there was clearly a shortage of men and the law was abolished. They were married in 1921. Thus, my uncle became my stepfather, and I soon had a younger brother for company.

For many years I wondered if I was the youngest orphan of the disaster, but since going to the conventions I have discovered other people such as Ellen Mary Walker. Over the years I've also had the pleasure of meeting some other survivors. Millvina Dean is a charming lady, full of vitality, and it is always delightful meeting up with her at *Titanic*-related events. Her after-dinner speech at the 1995 British Titanic Convention brought the house down. She did a repeat performance this year.

I have some rather poignant mementos of my father, which my mother passed on to me. His body was recovered by the cable ship *Mackay Bennett*, which had been chartered specifically for the purpose of recovering the dead.'

Here are the bald facts taken down by the embalmers on board the *Bennett* after Sidney Sedunary's corpse was laid out on the deck:

'No 178 – MALE – ESTIMATED AGE 25. BROWN HAIR. LIGHT MOUSTACHE.

CLOTHING – Blue serge suit; black boots and socks; uniform coat and waistcoat, with buttons.

TATTOO ON RIGHT ARM – Anchor and rose.

EFFECTS – Gold ring; knife; nickel watch; pawn ticket; pipe; ship's keys; 20s; $1.40; 8 francs 50.

NO MARKS ON CLOTHING.'

Sid continues:

'After identifying him and collecting his personal belongings he was buried at sea. My mother then received his few possessions in the post. His pocket watch still shows the time as 1.50am, which may well have been when he went into the water. Also returned were the keys to his cabin – number 45 on F deck – which he shared with the ship's interpreter, L. Muller. It is often forgotten that many people travelling in third class did not speak English as a first language, so after leaving Southampton Mr Muller must have been kept jolly busy.'

For Messrs Muller and Sedunary things had become much more complicated when the *Titanic* had reached Cherbourg:

'There was confusion rather than grumbling among the 102 "continental" passengers arriving at Cherbourg. They were Syrian, Croatian, Armenian and other Middle East nationals who, for reasons best known to their travel agents, had been routed from eastern Mediterranean ports via Marseilles to Paris and, now, to Cherbourg. Their travel arrangements called for departure via "the first available ship", and they were surprised and pleased to find themselves about to board *Titanic*.'

Titanic: Triumph and Tragedy, Eaton and Haas

It had been chaotic enough at Southampton and now the process of third class embarkation was repeated once again:

'Each passenger's ticket was stamped with the section letter. After being directed – and perhaps re-directed, several times – to the appropriate section, the passenger was shown to his or her berth. The considerable confusion among the 497 third class passengers boarding at Southampton may well be imagined. After the harassed stewards had helped their bewildered charges locate their berths, they turned to assist other incoming passengers...'

Eaton and Haas

A little of Sid's father's whereabouts after the collision on the night of the 14th can be ascertained from the evidence of third class steward John Hart at the British Inquiry held immediately after the disaster. Hart's answers reveal that an assistant, 'one by the name of Sedunary', was seen heading aft to ensure that the third class passengers in his care were provided with lifebelts. Interpreter Muller was later observed heading forward to the bow where the single men were quartered. He may well have had his assistant with him. Whatever the evidence, we can see plenty of activity below decks, with a number of industrious stewards attempting to aid and soothe the nerves of worried passengers. But as we know, Sidney Sedunary was not able to save himself. Sid continues his story:

'I donated the keys and watch to the Southampton Maritime Museum some years ago so that they could be enjoyed for future generations. However, I did keep some of his effects here: I have his smoking pipe, which is quite a bulky thing and must have been kept in his coat pocket; his wedding ring, which is tiny – he was only five foot four and slightly built; and a letter written by my mother, which he had on him at the time. It's incredibly well preserved. People love to touch the pipe and wedding ring, and by the way they handle them you'd think they were the Crown Jewels!

I saw *A Night To Remember* with my wife back in the 1950s. It was interesting to watch, but it didn't effect me particularly in any significant way. You see, there just wasn't the interest in it that there is today. We had endured two World Wars after the *Titanic* and people had other things on their minds. As for the latest instalment [James Cameron's film], it's just a love story that happens to be set on the

Titanic – there's nothing much more to say about it. However, the ship is recreated in a spectacular fashion and is fascinating to observe – a technological wonder. While I enjoyed the film for what it was, I believe *A Night To Remember* is more accurate. Coincidentally, Kate Winslet [star of Cameron's *Titanic*] was married in the same church as I was – she's a Reading girl, too!

As for salvaging things from the real wreck, I don't disagree with that if the items brought up are not sold privately and are displayed with care and sensitivity. The Greenwich Maritime Museum did a wonderful job with their exhibition and it was all tastefully done. I do think it will be a mistake to try and retrieve things from *within* the wreck – after all, it's one thing to pick plates and bags off the sea bed, but going inside the shattered hull to collect artefacts would be a foolishly risky operation.

The *Titanic* had never been a great influence on my life until 1985 when Robert Ballard discovered the wreck. Suddenly there seemed to be a veritable explosion of interest all over the world. Like many other people I read the newspapers with interest, but I didn't get fully involved until a bit later.

In 1992 I went to my first convention in Southampton, which coincidentally also happened to be the 80th anniversary of the disaster, and it absolutely amazed me! It was the day after the General Election but it was completely ignored. The only thing on everyone's mind was the *Titanic*. I had no idea so many people were interested in it – young and old. It really struck me when I saw a lady leafing through an old copy of *Sphere* [a period magazine detailing the events of the disaster] and showing such obvious reverence for the material. I mean, she was holding it as though it were an icon or something! On the second day the general public were allowed to view the memorabilia on display and the people wouldn't stop coming! That was when I fully understood the impact the *Titanic* has made over the last century. There is truly something captivating about it, and it's hard to explain why.

One man at the convention even asked me to sign a book for him. I was of course honoured to do so, but thought it incredible that anyone would want *my* signature! I suppose I am one of the few people with any sort of direct link with the ship, being one of the original *Titanic* orphans. There are so few survivors left today and only one or two of them get actively involved with the conventions – so I appear to be in demand!

I would never have written a book about the *Titanic* if it weren't for the continual interest in the disaster. I'm always busy these days attending openings and conventions, and it's always delightful meeting like-minded individuals. I've even made a model of the ship, which I'm rather proud of – though the air was blue at times during its construction!'

ANDREA DORIA
(1956)

9 July 2003

An e-mail from Pierette Simpson who hopes that I have received the account of her experiences on the *Andrea Doria* when it sank on 25 July 1956. I have it before me as I write and I'm very pleased with it. Pierette Simpson is a school teacher in Detroit, USA, and asked me if I could make use of a manuscript she wrote some years ago. I e-mailed her back immediately to accept her generous offer.

The Italian Line had suffered considerable losses during the course of the Second World War. Gone were the magnificent *Rex* and *Conti de Savioa* and gone too, it seemed, were all the former glories of the past. However, during the early 1950s the Italian Line regained much of its reputation with two sleek and ultra-modern ships. The *Andrea Doria* and *Christoforo Colombo* did not pretend to be high-speed competitors in the Atlantic race, but instead provided a service where style and a class A service were at a premium. Many observers noted how both ships were fitted out with cutting-edge design features and a wealth of specially commissioned artwork.

Launched in 1953, the *Andrea Doria* undertook the leisurely Genoa-Cannes-Naples-Gibraltar-New York run. In addition to its first class passengers, she also carried a large proportion of immigrants in 'tourist' class. One of these was Pierette Simpson who, as a young girl, found herself on board the *Andrea Doria* with her grandparents bound for America to join her mother and father who had already found work in Detroit.

At 11.10pm, on the final leg of her voyage, the *Andrea Doria* collided with the Swedish liner *Stockholm* in foggy weather near the Nantucket Lightship. The *Stockholm* ploughed into the *Andrea Doria*'s starboard side, her ice-strengthened bow piercing the Italian liner's double-bottomed tanks. Most of the *Andrea Doria*'s 47 victims were killed during the initial moment of impact.

The *Andrea Doria* took on an instant 18-degree list, which rendered her eight port-side lifeboats useless. This left only eight usable lifeboats for the 1,663 passengers and crew. An SOS was transmitted, but there was no announcement made to abandon ship as her commander, Captain Calamai, feared a stampede. Even so, without much communication between those in command and the passengers in their care there were inevitably scenes of consternation, panic and hysteria as the *Andrea Doria* slowly but inexorably rolled over deeper and deeper into the water.

Some ships in the area appeared to offer assistance, including the fine old French liner *Ile de France*. The *Stockholm*, badly damaged at the bow, remained afloat and also took on board survivors. Though unwilling to leave the stricken vessel, Captain Calamai finally abandoned the *Andrea Doria* in the early morning, and by 5.30am the ship was deserted. Because the wreck site was well attended by rescue ships, hundreds of witnesses were able to observe the new pride of the Italian Line turn over and disappear in a cloud of smoke and bubbles. An ugly court battle ensued between the Italian and Swedish-American lines, neither of whom would accept responsibility. Finally, in January 1957, both parties reached an out-of-court settlement.

Every year it seemed that a new set of students would want to hear how their teacher escaped from the *Andrea Doria*, so she finally decided to write down her experiences for them in a memoir she entitled 'My American Dream'. Apparently, the students refer to it as 'Miss Simpson's Titanic'.

PIERETTE SIMPSON

❝ I am an immigrant from Northern Italy, near the French border at the foot of the Alps. I was born in a village of about 100 inhabitants who farmed for a living, lived in homes without plumbing and sent their children to a one-room school house. The only toy I remember was a corn doll, which I made from an ear of corn that I picked in the fields, to which I added facial features with different colours of berries, then wrapped it in rags for clothing. Otherwise we climbed trees, played hide-and-seek in tall grasses, and I played my harmonica as I strolled the streets of the village. Because we were relatively poor by American standards, we knew that in order to make a better life for ourselves, we would have to relocate. Everyone had known for decades that America was the land where dreams were realised, if only one worked very hard.

My mother and father emigrated to Detroit in the early 1950s. Their plan was to work and buy a house so that my grandparents and I would join then later. After agonising for a long time about moving far from home, especially since we didn't speak English and had no marketable skills, we decided to emigrate to Detroit to join my parents.

In July 1956 we embarked for America, so that we too could partake in the American dream. We reserved three places aboard the *Andrea Doria*, the jewel of the Italian merchant fleet. At a cost of $29 million, the ship had taken more that nine million man hours to construct, and, thanks to the latest technology, it was designed to be unsinkable. By all standards, it was considered the thirteenth greatest ship in all history.

As we left port, I remember being overcome with joy, as this 30,000-ton queen and its ten storeys of grandeur carried me to my dreams. My grandparents were fearful of such a long voyage, but their anxiety soon turned to wonder as we marvelled at many of its unique features. For one, the ship was the showcase of Italy's best artists and artisans, exhibiting wall tapestries, crystal-cut mirrors and fine silverwork. We had never visited a museum before, and certainly not a floating one. Each day's routine included swimming in the pool and dining in the luxurious dining hall. The tables were covered with decorative ice sculptures and an abundant assortment of beautifully prepared dishes. How different this was from the daily diet of fried beans and potatoes prepared on a black wood-burning stove that stood in my humble village kitchen. Each day was a floating feast and we were relaxed enough after a few days to enjoy it for the rest of the week.

It was 25 July, the eve of our landing. As is part of the Italian culture, such an occasion calls for serious celebration. Many passengers assembled in the elegant ballroom for dancing. We had much to be joyous about – after one glorious week at sea, we would see the shores of the promised land!

As fate would have it, at 11.20pm our merriment was abruptly terminated by a sudden jolt. I remember clearly the sound of hundreds of bottles crashing from the bar, smashing to the floor and walls. We were flung in every direction by a force that overpowered even those of us who were hanging on to railings and anchored tables. Though the ship seemed to have come to a complete halt, the furniture continued to slide to one side, the starboard side, which was listing sharply. Among cries from broken limbs and separation from loved ones came the realisation that we were sinking. There had been a terrible collision, but how? With what? We worked swiftly to try to balance the wounded queen by pushing heavy furniture to the high side in an effort to balance it. We worked to the point of desperate exhaustion and despair. No on knew yet that the *Andrea Doria* had been struck by another ship, the *Stockholm*. In the thick fog of the night, the *Stockholm* had misread radar calculations and managed to carve its path through one third of the *Andrea Doria*. Then, as it retreated, it managed to leave a clear path for the ocean waters to swell inside the cabins occupied just minutes before by sleeping immigrants. Several passengers were killed immediately by the twisting of mangled steel, others soon died of serious wounds, and the more fortunate ones made their way through the corridors filled with smoke and with water in order to reach the upper decks. My grandfather was one of the fortunate ones. One young passenger, a girl whose yellow pyjamas were smeared with blood, managed to find herself on the bow of the *Stockholm*, and was able to speak to a cleaning man, without a clue as to how she had been transported there. Fortunately, the *Stockholm* was not sinking.

On the *Andrea Doria*, hours had passed and the only recourse that remained was prayer, and pray we did while sitting on the ballroom floor, winding rosary beads through our fingers. After what seemed like an eternity, a man appeared at the door leading to the deck. His face filled with promise for salvation, he announced loudly, 'Lifeboats are here to rescue us! Women and children first.' He explained that all the men would be tying ropes around our waists and lowering us into the lifeboats. At last there was hope that not all our dreams would have been in vain. We lined up on the slippery deck, careful not to slide down and fall into the ocean. A little girl did fall into the sea. Fortunately, her mother was an Olympic diver and she rescued her daughter by diving in after her. I patiently awaited my turn and then I felt the tight rope being wound around my waist. My grandmother was crying as I was lowered into what seemed to be a very overcrowded lifeboat. Seasickness overcame many of us. My grandmother was lowered right after me. Her feet slipped into the water as she tried to reach the sides of the small swaying vessel. She sat terrified as we began to row quickly in the black, shark-infested waters littered with debris from the accident.

Our lifeboat was in danger of being sucked into a whirlpool made by the giant ship. We finally arrived at our rescue ship, the *Ile de France*. But we were not out of danger yet because we still had to climb up several decks on narrow rope ladders over what seemed like a black abyss below. When we reached the top of the rope ladder, someone pulled us through the small window and covered us with warm blankets as we made our way toward a large hall that had been converted into a comfort room. I fell asleep next to my grandmother soon afterwards. I don't know when my grandfather arrived but fortunately he had also been brought to the *Ile de France*, rather than on the of the other rescue ships that encircled us from a distance.

Early next morning we landed on what truly seemed like the promised land! Families had gathered to welcome the shocked and exhausted passengers of the *Andrea Doria*. Most of the passengers were immigrants who had dreamed of this moment, although the script of the film they had played in their minds had been changed dramatically by fate. The loudspeakers announced the names of survivors as they arrived. It was ecstasy for some families and agony for others as they discovered that their loved ones had been killed in a collision during the night, just twenty miles from the shores of Nantucket. Those poor souls who had left their old world behind, betting that the new world would bring them closer to their dreams, never had their chance to fulfil them!

Fortunately, my grandparents and I had reached our destination. But our dreams seemed shattered. We had lost everything, except the clothes on our back. After the shock subsided, we realised that there was only one thing to do and that was to keep focused on our goals. We had at last reached the land of opportunity and in the face of such insurmountable odds we soon found work in a lumber yard, and my grandmother worked as a seamstress. I went to school. I studied diligently while I tried to learn English and make new friends. But children laughed as I struggled with words. They teased me about my old tattered clothes, which were hand-me-downs from neighbours, and they snickered at my strange ways of doing things, like taking a half-hour just to eat a sandwich. With the same strong determination that my grandfather used to guide the plough behind the ox in the fields of my native land, I pushed forward. As soon as I became a naturalised citizen I began to focus on my future. Happily, two of my greatest desires, wanting to become an accomplished violinist and a foreign language teacher, were realised.

GENERAL SLOCUM
(1904)

19 September 2003

A small package arrived today from America. Inside was a cassette tape labelled simply 'Adella'. I popped it into the machine and pressed play. The lady who spoke next sounded weak but I could, however, discern the clear accent of a New Yorker: 'My name is Adella Leibenow Wotherspoon and I am a survivor of the *General Slocum* disaster.'

To me, 1904 is a sepia world of trams, waxed moustaches, telegrams and bustles. An era far back in time. Therefore I had resigned myself to having to research personal testimonies of the *General Slocum* disaster from archival material. Then, in mid-2003, I was amazed to read about the existence of the one last remaining survivor of the tragedy. Here was someone who could open a window into that sepia world for me and colour it with her own memories. Hoping against hope, I contacted Mrs Wotherspoon, enquiring if she would tell me her story. To my delight she agreed.

On 15 June 1904 the morning sun was shining as a wooden sidewheel steamboat, the *General Slocum*, pulled out from its East Third Street pier in Lower Manhattan. On board were more than 1,300 residents of the Lower East Side, an enclave called Little Germany, or 'Kleindeutschland'. The ship had been chartered by members of St Mark's Lutheran church on East Sixth Street for their annual picnic to Long Island Sound. The mood on board was merry and cheerful. For many of the hardworking day-trippers, this was going to be a rare chance to relax and forget about the worries of life. St Mark's Reverend George Haas cast his watchful gaze over his flock, happy in the knowledge that everyone aboard was enjoying themselves.

As the *General Slocum* was passing through Hell Gate, an inferno suddenly enveloped the wooden ship. Since there had been no fire drill on board, nobody knew what to do. Inexperienced crew members wrestled with leaking fire hoses, aghast at their useless condition, and hundreds of passengers flung themselves into the river. Some were swept under and drowned in the strong current, others plummeted to the bottom of the river bed, weighed down by aged life-preservers filled not with buoyant cork but dusty cork grains. There was no chance to escape in the lifeboats, as they had been inexplicably affixed to the deck.

Captain William Van Shaick headed the *General Slocum* into the wind for about a mile, fanning the smoke and flames back into the ship's superstructure, before beaching the blistering wreck on North Brother Island. Passengers were pushed to the stern by the flames and many who could not swim suffered the indescribable torture of being burned alive. Others who took their chances in the river drowned in only a few feet of water, well within sight of land. Everywhere it seemed there were the lifeless bodies of men, women and children, and the acrid smell of scorched paint, hair and charred flesh. The air was filled with a cacophony of screams, sobbing and cries of disbelief as the decks of the *General Slocum* collapsed down into the hull, crushing the bodies of those still strapped inside.

Around 1,021 people died, of whom 93 were missing, never to be recovered, and 42 were too disfigured through submersion and decomposition to be identified. Thirty-eight victims were burned so severely that the recovery team failed to recognise any discernible human features. Moreover, 15 children were orphaned by the loss of both parents. A relief fund was begun and within a few days it had raised $9,000. One reporter from *World* wrote, 'Never again will I believe our city has no heart.'

Funeral parlours and morgues were overwhelmed with the dead, and staff had to work overtime to keep up with the dramatic increase in demand for their services. It seemed as if all of Little Germany had gone into mourning. There were scenes of unparalleled hysteria and grief in the streets and some of the bereaved took their own lives by casting themselves into the East River.

Though badly injured in the fire, Captain Van Shaick was still sentenced to ten years in Sing Sing for his conduct. However, it was widely felt that he was a scapegoat. The Knickerbocker Steamboat Company was sharply criticised for allowing a patently unseaworthy vessel a licence to carry passengers. In due course the company president and its directors were all found guilty of criminal negligence. It was a small comfort for the survivors, but it didn't bring back all those men, women and children.

ADELLA WOTHERSPOON

66 My mother and father were Paul and Anna Leibenow. I was born in Little Germany on 28 November 1903. My father was a bartender and had done well enough to move us all out of Little Germany (or 'Kleindeutschland' as it was known to us) up to Harlem, which in those days was a very up and coming neighbourhood. However, they still had strong ties with St Mark's Lutheran church, so the trip on the *General Slocum* was a bit like a reunion with old friends.

It was a real family occasion because as well as my mother and father and myself – a babe in arms – there were my sisters Helen, aged six, and Anna, aged three. My father's two sisters, Annie and Martha, were also coming along. Aunt Annie was married to Frank Weber, and they lived in Little Germany at that time. They also brought their two children Emma, aged eleven, and Frank Jr, aged seven. Aunt Martha was unmarried, but she came along to help out because I'm sure mother and Aunt Annie had their hands full! It was rare in those days to get much time off work, so Uncle Frank and my father must have been looking forward to the trip immensely. Later on Aunt Annie said that everyone was so happy boarding that boat. She said everyone was laughing and talking and the children were romping about. They chatted to Pastor Haas from St Mark's and eagerly found some seats on deck. The weather was beautiful and it looked like it was going to be a wonderful day out.

I don't think anybody really knew what caused the fire. Apparently it started in the lamp room below the main deck. Whatever it was, it certainly spread quickly. Aunt Martha had decided to take Anna and Helen to get an ice-cream on the deck below. Emma and cousin Frank begged to go too. She told my mother and father that they wouldn't be long. 'We'll be right back,' she said. I expect my parents were glad to get a break! Off they went, all laughing and joking. They were never seen again. They got caught up in the fire that suddenly engulfed the lower deck. All of them perished.

It seemed that my parents didn't notice the fire until a little time later. My Aunt Annie said, 'It was a big puff of smoke which startled everyone but someone said it must have been something burning in the kitchen and we just laughed it off. But then there was a sheet of flame which appeared from nowhere and everyone panicked.' My parents were desperate to know what had become of the children. My father and Uncle Frank dashed down to the deck below where the smoke was already very thick, while my mother clutched hold of me. I simply can't imagine what was going through her mind.

My father got separated from Uncle Frank, so he decided to return to find my mother and Aunt Annie. He brought with him some life-preservers so that it would give us a chance in the water. The life-preservers were hung about eight feet above the deck and my father recalled seeing dozens of people reaching up desperately trying to get them, arms straining. He later said that many of them were actually wired in place and it took him some time to pull them free.

Meanwhile Uncle Frank and some other men were trying to free up some of the lifeboats, but again they wouldn't budge because they were tied down and secured with wire. Nothing they could do would shift them so they had to simply leave them. He said the speed with which the decks were burning was incredible, but even so he saw some people actually rushing *into* the flames trying to find their children.

I have no idea how I was saved – it was a miracle really. My mother had held me in her arms and jumped on to a tugboat that had come to our rescue. Her left side and arm were badly burned where she had shielded me from the heat. She was put down on to the beach at North Brother Island and sat there in shock. She had no idea what had happened to my father and my sisters or the rest of the family. There were bodies floating about in the water and bodies laid out on the beach. An hysterical woman came up to her and demanded that my mother gave back 'her baby'. My mother said, 'What sex is your baby?' and the woman told her it was a boy, whereby my mother gently told her the baby she had in her arms was a girl. The poor woman must have been half mad with grief and ran off. Then suddenly my father appeared with Aunt Annie and Uncle Frank. It was a tragic time for them because they didn't know what had happened to their children – they had no idea if they were alive or dead. So Uncle Frank and my father set off again to find them.

Later on they went to the morgue, but they couldn't find any of the children, so they headed off for the hospitals. My mother, myself and Aunt Annie were taken to the Lebanon Hospital to get over the shock and to recover from our injuries. Aunt Annie wasn't in a very good condition because the smoke had damaged her lungs. They both must have worried dreadfully about their children, and it can't have helped their state of mind.

The next day my father and Uncle Frank knew it was all over. They had waited for the tugs bringing in the dead all day and night but it was hopeless. My father actually brought some black armbands from the local store because he had lost hope. The body of my sister Anna was later found, but Helen was gone – missing for ever – as was my cousin Emma. Some time later my cousin Frank's body was recovered, but he was barely recognisable and was only identified by his clothing. He was buried in the family plot.

The whole of Little Germany went into mourning. Nearly everyone was affected by tragedy because it was such a small, tight-knit community. The church was certainly a great support and comfort to people, but even so many people simply took their own life because they couldn't come to terms with their loss. At the enquiry my father was called and he testified about the appalling condition of the life-preservers and the fact that they were wired in place. He still had badly cut hands and showed them to the jury as proof of his efforts. Ultimately it was revealed that the *General Slocum* was completely unsafe and should never have been allowed to put out to sea. However, it wasn't much comfort to those people who were still grieving their dead. No amount of questions would ever bring them back.

A year later, on 15 June 1905, my parents took me to the memorial service at the Lutheran cemetery in Queens. My parents were still grief-stricken and wore their mourning clothes. My mother dressed me in a new white dress because I had been chosen by the Organisation of the General Slocum Survivors to unveil a new monument in honour of the sixty-one unidentified dead. Later on we took a trolley car to the cemetery in Middle Village for a service there. I, of course, had no idea what was going on, and mother said that I babbled away and enjoyed myself. Poor Aunt Annie and

Uncle Frank were there too, and it must have been an awful strain for them.

My father carried on working as a bartender in Harlem and took wonderful care of my mother and me. He decided that he would record as much as he could about the disaster so that I could read about it and understand when I got older. He purchased a scrapbook and started to paste articles into it about the *General Slocum*. The first entries dealt with the anniversary of the disaster – and coincidentally there were many photographs of myself as the 'Youngest Slocum Survivor' opening the monument. Later on he started to add anything relating to steamboat safety at sea, including reforms. Some of the *General Slocum* items are very sad, such as the envelopes from the morgue that held the personal effects of cousins Frank and Emma. Emma's envelope has the inscription: 'Emma Weber, Body 765, Ring-diamond clip. Sterling Silver Chain bracelet – charred.' You see, he wanted me to know everything about it. There are letters he wrote to the Department of Charities asking about Helen's missing body, a sweet photograph of Helen when she was alive, receipts for his mourning band, poems, everything. He did it for four years. It was his way of making sense of it all, his therapy.

Titanic threads...
Tea with grandmother

Sunday. Popped in to see my grandmother. Like her older brothers and sisters (she was one of ten) she laces everything with humour. I think it's got something to do with her tough northern upbringing (picture Gracie Fields or Catherine Cookson and you've got the idea...).

Last week she asked me how my research was going. 'What's it about again?' she asks. 'Something to do with the *Titanic*?'

I ask her what she thinks of the *Titanic* disaster in general. 'Haven't ever given it much thought,' she says with finality, and would I like another cup of tea? The subject is closed. Sometimes it's a relief talking to someone who couldn't give a hoot.

DUCHESS OF ATHOLL
(1942)

22 October 2003

It struck me today reading through two accounts I have been sent about the sinking of the *Duchess of Atholl* that shipping lines loved to give their vessels very grand titles. I wonder if the *real* Duchess of Atholl liked having a ship named after her? Probably she did, but then it must have given her a queer feeling when she found out it had sunk. Shivers down the spine, I should think.

The Canadian Pacific Line had already lost a considerable amount of tonnage, including two of its flagships, *Empress of Asia* and *Empress of Britain*, when their smaller cousin, the *Duchess of Atholl*, was destroyed in late 1942. Built in 1928 for the Liverpool-Montreal run, the *Duchess of Atholl* was commandeered by the British Admiralty as a troopship in December 1939. At 601 feet long and with two funnels, she was an aesthetically pleasing vessel capable of carrying 1,570 passengers in three classes.

Sailing as part of a convoy from Cape Town to the UK via Freetown, the *Duchess of Atholl* was loaded with troops and women and children when it was torpedoed 200 miles east of Ascension Island by U-178. As part of its cargo manifest the ship was ferrying much-needed supplies of fresh fruit and vegetables back to a rationed British public. When one of the torpedoes pierced the hold it appeared as if the sky was raining oranges – a colourful and no doubt sticky finale to the *Duchess of Atholl*'s career. Four crew members were killed in the initial attack and the other survivors were picked up by ships in the convoy.

Contemporary newspaper reports highlighted the 'calm courage and discipline' of the children, which inspired the 'hardened British seamen':

'All the seamen would talk about was the splendid conduct of the little ones. They did not panic. They smiled. Entering the lifeboats they behaved as if they were going on a new kind of picnic. Like a well-disciplined army they carried out orders given from the bridge.'

Unsurprisingly, no mention was made of the equally splendid conduct of the Captain of U-178, who had ignored the 'Laconia Order' and whose civility and appearance made a distinct impression on young Mavis Mackay and Private S. G. Millington.

MAVIS MACKAY

“ My mother and I were coming back to England, having been evacuated abroad to Malta. We flew to Cairo first, but then decided to join my father in Alexandria. He was a tug master there, so he was unable to come with us. We boarded the *Duchess of Atholl* at Cape Town after a long and protracted journey. She was nicknamed 'the rolling Duchess', and as I was a dreadful sailor I was seasick most of the time. Then, between Cape Town and Freetown on 10 August, we were woken up out of our bunks by an explosion that rocked the whole ship. My mother, sister and I dressed and went up on deck, but we were told that it was only trouble in the engine room so we went back to our cabins.

There followed a second explosion, and a steward started shouting 'Boat Decks!', which we knew meant for everyone to go to the lifeboat stations. After putting on our lifejackets we went up on deck and were told to climb into the lifeboats. I remember crying because I had left my doll behind, and a sailor offering to go and get if for me. Of course, my mother was furious with me and he didn't go. However, my mother remembered a lady going to the bathroom just before the second explosion and the sailor went back for her – as she had apparently been locked in.

The lifeboats were lowered and the adults were told to row as quickly as possible away from the ship. Then the third torpedo was fired into the ship's hold, where it blew up a load of oranges. The sky was just full of orange pieces. We watched the ship sink and I have remembered that moment all my life. I was terrified as I could not swim.

I can't remember how long into Saturday it was, but some time during the day a German submarine surfaced and the Captain made himself known. Oddly, what sticks out in my mind even today is his red hair, which was quite striking. He asked for the name of the ship and where the Captain and first officers were. He then instructed everyone to stand up, and although the adults stood up, we children were told by our parents to lie down. The Germans then took photographs of everyone and asked if anyone needed medical attention. The submarine then submerged and only came back up again once in the evening. My mother told us that the reason we children were told to lay down was that they thought they were going to be shot, as apparently the day before it had been announced over the radio that no survivors were to be left – but obviously the German Captain was more humane. We were in the lifeboats all day Saturday and the following night too. We had ship's biscuits (like bricks!) to eat and some water. One or two lifeboats had chocolate, but we didn't.

The next day we were singing hymns, as we had the Padre in our lifeboat, when someone spotted a flying-boat on the horizon, so of course everyone was shouting and waving. During the night, although the lifeboats were told to keep together, they drifted apart, but the plane circled around us. Then sometime later a corvette called the *Corinthian* appeared. When the ship came close to each lifeboat we had to climb a rope ladder to get on board. I remember I had a small bag with me, which contained my mother's jewellery, but as the handle had broken one of the men in our boat offered to carry it for me. When I reached the deck the man was nowhere to be seen. My mother reported this to the captain who found the bag later but it was empty. The man said he had put the bag down as soon as he reached the deck. Naturally my mother was furious that anyone could stoop so low during such a dreadful time.

We slept in the sailor's bunks and they slept on the deck (as did my mother), because there were so many of us there wasn't much room on such a small ship. We were taken to Freetown where we were transferred to another ship, the *Neahelus*. I remember it pouring with rain and we were getting drenched. When we reached the ship a message was sent out on the radio about us survivors being wet through and all we had was what we stood up in. Later, the people of Freetown brought clothes for us to wear.

We then travelled to Scotland. Later on we made our way to Portsmouth by train and I can remember remarking to my mother how like doll's-houses the houses looked along the way – only to be told that we would be living in one! To rub salt in the wound, we were told we could apply to the WVS for clothes, but were informed that the clothes were for bombed-out victims of the British Isles and they wanted proof of our misfortunes. Thus, we received nothing at all from them. What a way to end it!

S. G. MILLINGTON

❝I was having a lie-in on the morning the *Duchess* was attacked. I had to get up for work at 6.00am, but as I had half an hour to go I turned over for a few more minutes of sleep when suddenly there was a terrific explosion.

Our quarters were off the working alleyway opposite the entrance to the engine room. The first torpedo hit the engine room, killing an engineer and four engine room ratings. It also destroyed all the electrics on board and the ship was plunged into darkness and all appliances were rendered useless.

The force of the explosion blew our cabin door off and the room was filled with cordite fumes. As you can imagine, I was out of my bed in a flash! My shorts and shoes were damaged so I just rushed up to the deck half-dressed.

I looked around, but couldn't see anyone. There was then another explosion as we had been hit by another torpedo. By word of mouth we were instructed to close the watertight doors by hand. This was done of course, but the ship was listing in the water. We were then ordered to Emergency Stations and all passengers and crew were standing by at these on the boat deck.

The submarine then fired another torpedo. About on hour had passed since we were first hit and the ship was listing more and more. The Captain gave the order to abandon ship just as another torpedo crashed into the hull.

The lifeboats were manned and the ship was abandoned. We were about 50 yards from the *Duchess*, which by this time had a bad list to port. On the forward well deck a lifeboat had become jammed on the falls and there were about twelve RAF personnel trying to free it. The officer on my lifeboat could see they were in trouble and he asked for volunteers to go back to the ship and help to get the boat away. Half a dozen men in my lifeboat volunteered and we proceeded back to the ship.

We climbed up the Jacob's Ladder and reached the deck and started to free the boat from the falls. While we were doing this the submarine put another torpedo right underneath us into the forward hold. We were carrying a cargo of potatoes and oranges and the force of the explosion blew the top of the hatch clear away and thousands of oranges rained down over us. The sky was totally orange for a few seconds.

By this time the ship had listed half over on its side and it looked as if she would go at any time. One of the crew said, 'This is the third time I've been sunk and I'm off!' He scrambled down and I followed close behind.

In my haste I missed a rung and down I plummeted into the sea. Falling like that was terrifying because I knew that right below me was a torpedo hole and if it was on the side where I entered the water I wouldn't surface – for the suction would have drawn me down. Much to my relief I went down about six feet before surfacing.

I swam to the lifeboat and was pulled aboard. Having swallowed some fuel I was then very sick. After recovering a bit I looked at the *Duchess* and could see she wouldn't last long. She was practically capsized and smoke and steam were belching from her funnels. She then gave a shudder and started to slide stem first into the depths.

When she had completely disappeared the submarine that had sunk her surfaced. The submarine crew appeared on deck manning the guns and trained them on the lifeboats. Then the Captain appeared on deck. We expected him to give out an order to fire on us but he simply asked us the name of the ship he had sunk and where we were bound for and where we had come from. He also wanted to know where our Captain was, as he was obliged to take him prisoner. He apologised for sinking us but said simply that it was 'War'. He also said that he knew we had got a radio distress signal off and it would not be long before we were picked up. With that, he submerged and left us.

So there we were in open boats exposed to the tropical sun. After 36 hours in the lifeboats we were picked up by an armed cruiser (resembling nothing more than an old banana boat) which took us to Freetown. There we were put aboard the armed cruiser *Carnarvon Castle* for transportation back to England. On board there were three other ships' crews and passengers who had been sunk just like us.

23 October 2003

A treat waiting on my e-mail this morning from the Eastland Disaster Historical Society. There are only four living survivors of this American shipwreck and one of them, Marion Eichholz, is happy to give her account to me for my journal. Although she was only a child at the time and her memories are limited, I am delighted to be able to include them here.

The *Eastland* disaster of 24 July 1915 is unusual for two reasons: first, because it concerns a maritime tragedy that happened while the ship was practically in port, and second, because until relatively recently very few people had even heard of it. Yet, remarkably, more than 800 people were killed – including a staggering 22 entire families.

The Western Electric Company of Chicago had chartered the *Eastland*, an excursion boat, to take its employees on their annual picnic across Lake Michigan to Michigan City, Indiana. The *Eastland* was nicknamed the 'speed queen of the Great Lakes' and was a popular ship. However, her service record was worryingly erratic.

During one crossing in 1904, with several thousand on board, she suddenly heeled to starboard, righted herself and lurched immediately to port. The crew acted quickly and shunted the passengers deep into the hull, where the lower centre of gravity prevented her from rolling inexorably over. Several thousand citizens of St Joseph witnessed the event, and damaging word of mouth soon cut into her business. Despite this, the *Eastland* was often used by companies to take their staff on excursions – although, a few years before the final disaster, the ship had nearly capsized completely during a Sherwin Williams Paint Company day trip.

An estimated 7,000 tickets had been sold for the Western Electric Company picnic, and on the morning of 24 July 1915 the *Eastland* was filling with excited and eager passengers looking forward to a well-earned day off. Predictably, the ship started to list with a slow roll to starboard and then again to port. Some of the passengers thought it was a lark and didn't realise the potential danger ahead.

However, this time the *Eastland* kept going and capsized by her dock at the Clark Street Bridge. There were roughly 2,500 passengers on board – though a complete list has never been established. Most died within seconds, trapped inside the hull, while others barely got their feet wet. Once again, as with the *General Slocum* disaster, a community went into mourning.

MARION EICHHOLZ

❝July 24th 1915 was a very tragic day in Cicero. It was the day of the *Eastland* disaster. I remember only a few incidents of that day. My Mom, Anna Eichholz, and my Dad, Fred Eichholz, were seated on the upper deck and I was standing by Mom's chair. Mom pulled me back to her side. She began yelling, 'Run to the other side of the boat!' People began to panic, and women were running and screaming. Dad picked me up in his arms, stood on the railing and jumped into the river. I believe he told Mom to go to the other side of the boat, but because there was so much panic, Mom stayed in her seat. When the boat went over she floated from the seat into the water. Someone threw her a rope, and she was rescued. I remember Dad swimming with me in one arm. I was crying and my strap slippers were dangling from my ankles. We were picked up by a tugboat and brought to shore.

Some of those rescued were brought to some of the buildings near the river. Dad brought me to one of them and left me there while he went back home to put on dry clothes. He also planned to come back and look for Mom, as he was not certain whether she had survived. While he was getting into dry clothes, a car pulled up in front of the house, bringing mum home. Someone had sat me in a chair and put a man's suit coat over me. Here I fell sound asleep. But I do remember waking up when Dad and Mrs Lainge came. I do not recall the trip home at all, but I remember walking into the bedroom and Mom saying, 'Hello Marion,' and she sounded happy to see me again. Mrs Lainge stayed for a short while to talk and I played with her purse.

After this, a doctor from the Board of Health came several times to give us inoculations against typhoid fever. Once I saw him coming and ran to hide in the bedroom. But he was so nice and soothed my fears.

In those days, it was customary for the funeral director to hang a crepe on the front door where there was a deceased person. Pastor McCarrell said it seemed as if there was a crepe on almost every door in Cicero. The gates of the Western Electric Company were draped in black. A reporter came from one of the newspapers and took my picture in front of 4821 West 23rd Street. They wrote 'RESCUED' at the bottom of the picture.

Titanic threads...
Marjorie Newell

'Now made tired by the day,
So my ardent desire shall
warmly greet the starry night
like a tired child.'
'Beim schlafengehen', Hermann Hesse

Marjorie Newell Robb was 23 years old in 1912. Accompanied by her beloved father and older sister, she boarded the *Titanic* at Cherbourg. For the rest of her life she retained crystal clear memories of both the ship and the disaster that followed. She lived to the venerable age of 103 and in her later years she would often grant interviews to anyone with an interest.

In James Cameron's film, *Titanic*, Rose Calvert, a 101-year-old survivor, says, 'A woman's heart is a deep ocean of secrets.' Four women in the Newell family of Boston, USA, had their hearts broken by the *Titanic* disaster. Madeleine Crowley, Marjorie Newell Robb's daughter, told me that the impression the tragedy left on the family was so strong that it filtered through each generation, shading the lives of the women left behind.

'I never knew my mother had been on the *Titanic* until I was about twelve years old. She came to me one day with a letter someone had written to her about the *Titanic* saying, 'Your grandfather was a hero, it's all here for you to see.' I had no *idea* my mother had been on board, much less my grandfather. She wouldn't talk about it. It was just something that she wanted to forget. There was a large picture of my grandfather over the fireplace in my grandmother's house and whenever I asked her about him I would be told that he was a 'fine, noble man' and that he had been well respected. No more than that – no mention of the *Titanic*.

My grandmother Mary Newell was a true Victorian lady. After my grandfather was killed she went into mourning for the rest of her life. So we respected her wishes – as did my mother – and never spoke of

121

the *Titanic*. Right up until the end of her life in 1957 my grandmother was unshaken in her belief that the *Titanic* had ruined her life. It took many long years with lengthy silences in between for me to learn the story of what happened, the truth.

In 1912 my grandfather, Arthur Newell, had arranged a holiday for the family to North Africa and the Middle East. He was particularly interested in seeing the Holy Land and, being a devoted church-goer, who made a study of the Bible, it was a long-held ambition to see the ancient sites for himself. My grandmother and her middle daughter Alice had decided not to go because they were of a delicate constitution. So that left my mother Marjorie and the oldest sister, Madeleine (after whom I am named). The three of them enjoyed the holiday very much. Mother said that places such as Bethlehem and Jerusalem left a strong impression on her father and it moved him deeply.

It was a wonderful trip for my mother in other ways too. She even had an amorous adventure when in Cairo a dashing young man persistently pursued her. One night he appeared under her balcony on a white horse in order to "woo" her! How romantic! However, my grandfather said it was "indecent" and had him chased away.

Arthur could be a stem disciplinarian and a raised eyebrow or look could silence his children. Despite this, my mother loved and respected him very much. She often told me that it was a special honour when he asked her to go for a walk with him. He was a very busy man who had to deal with pressing business matters which always took up much of his time (in 1897 he had been elected chairman of the Fourth National Bank in Boston), yet he would always try to make time for his daughters. On these walks mother would listen enraptured to the stories he told her, thrilled to spend time alone with the man she loved and admired so much. She later mused that her grandfather was the "kingpin" of the family and all the women in the family deferred to him.

My mother was an energetic woman who loved outdoor pursuits such as hiking. Even in her later years she would be striding along with a purpose, full of vitality. However, she was also a keen musician and the family were, as a whole, passionate about music. All three sisters played the violin or viola, grandmother played the piano beautifully, and Arthur was a keen cellist. Every Sunday at home in Percy Street the family would play together, and it was a source of great joy to them all. The girls were taught by some of the best music instructors in Boston.

The return journey to America on the *Titanic* had been arranged by my grandfather as a surprise gift for the girls. Mother said that she and Madeleine were absolutely delighted in every way. They were very excited to be travelling home on the largest ship in the world – and on her maiden voyage! The trio boarded at Cherbourg in France as first class passengers and Marjorie said that the *Titanic* looked simply magnificent.

Mother remembered the *Titanic* so well. She told me that on the first night aboard she and Madeleine were waiting for their father at the foot of the grand staircase before going into dinner. That night she was wearing her first proper evening gown with a long train. Fifty years later her most vivid memory of that moment was hearing the distinct rustle of the ladies' silk dresses as they brushed down the steps.

After dinner the girls were introduced to the millionaire John Jacob Astor and his wife Madeleine in the reception room. Mrs Astor was younger than Mr Astor's son. This didn't impress my mother, who privately thought she was far too young. In her way, mother could be rather prim about matters like that – even though she was practically the same age as Mrs Astor at the time!

On the last day before the disaster mother told me that she and her father sat out on deck relaxing on the wooden steamer chairs discussing their recent sight-seeing expeditions. Arthur was impressed with everything he had seen. It made mother so proud to know she had shared these experiences with him.

At about 10.30pm the family went to bed. Mother could recall feeling the collision with the iceberg, which happened just over half an hour later. Arthur knocked at the door and told his daughters to put on their warmest clothes and follow him up to the deck. He tried to find out what had happened but there was a lot of confusion and no one seemed to be able to give him a clear answer. Mother remembered that at this point she could already feel the ship listing slightly.

Arthur took the girls out on to the boat deck and handed them into lifeboat 6. He thought it was dangerous for the women to go bobbing about in an open boat in the middle of the sea and would have preferred it if they had stayed on board where it seemed much safer. However, he told the girls that it was just a precaution and they would only have to lay off from the ship for a while until the damage was repaired. His last words to my mother were, 'We must obey orders,' and he was firm in his conviction that they should go. Naturally, both sisters obeyed. If their father insisted they go, then that's exactly what they would do. It never *occurred* to my mother that the ship would sink and that her dear father would be killed. There was no urgency about the situation you see, everything was calm. There hadn't been an explosion or a siren going off, no fire or smoke – nothing to say that the ship was in trouble at all. So at first everyone thought it was rather ridiculous to be getting into lifeboats in the middle of the night!

The last thing mother remembered of her father was seeing him stand back assisting the other women into the boat. She told me that she often wondered what had happened to him after that. But she knew that no matter what the situation on board, he would never have left the ship if there had been other women and children who needed help. It also occurred to her that he must have regretted taking his daughters on that trip.'

In a later interview Marjorie Newell described the *Titanic*'s final moments:

'From about a mile away we saw the *Titanic* sink. From the time we left her she was sinking slowly at the head but began to sink faster. The water got into the engine room for we heard a terrific explosion. The stern of the *Titanic* lifted way out of the water and the ship's keel showed. The tipping of the vessel threw everybody toward the bow and the ship went to the bottom.

It was cold and dark. The great ship made a tremendous groan and there was suddenly a great rush of water before she went down. I'll never forget that enormous, awful roar.'

Madeleine Crowley continues:

'When the two sisters reached New York a family friend was there to meet them as they disembarked from the *Carpathia*. My grandmother couldn't bear to come down so she stayed in a nearby hotel. It was a emotional reunion. She had expected to see the *three* of them and let out a piercing scream and nearly fainted when she saw it was only the two girls coming down the corridor. From that moment on, life was never the same.

Two weeks later the family was informed that Arthur's body had been recovered. He was shipped back to the United States and buried in Mount Auburn Cemetery in Cambridge, Massachusetts. The memorial service was overflowing with people wishing to pay their respects, and the congregation sang *Nearer My God to Thee*. Many moving tributes poured in over the forthcoming weeks. Thenceforth, *nobody* was to discuss the *Titanic* at home.

Like Queen Victoria, my grandmother wore black for nearly the rest of her days. She slept with Arthur's watch under her pillow. Grandmother would never have considered remarrying. She simply lived with the cherished memory of her dear husband until the day she died.

In 1917 my mother married and eventually had four children. My brother was named Arthur after my grandfather. Mother retained a love of music her whole life. I can recall her greatest joy was playing quartets and it was quite common to hear her performing at home when I was growing up in the 1920s and '30s. In later life she taught violin and piano at Wells College in Aurora, New York – something she derived great satisfaction from. Later still, she became one of the founders of the New Jersey Symphony Orchestra. Music was very much in her blood!

Aunt Madeleine never married and lived a quiet life at home. I admired her so because she was a graceful, selfless woman, very concerned about the well-being of her family and friends. She had a great interest in public affairs, both domestic and foreign, and was particularly concerned about humanitarian issues; any improvements in this field gave her great comfort. My aunt valued her privacy and that of her family and protected my grandmother from prying eyes and anything that might upset her. Like my mother, Aunt Madeleine went about fulfilling her duties both at home and in the community. She also enjoyed academic life and had attended Smith College at the turn of the century.'

However, she could never forget the *Titanic* disaster. In 1957 Madeleine broke her vow of silence when she wrote to her friend Marjorie Grey (referring to herself initially in the third person):

'Mr and Mrs Newell [her parents] had never been separated till he and Madeleine and her younger sister Marjorie took that trip to Europe in 1912 and came back on the *Titanic*. Mrs Newell and Alice, the middle sister, went on to New York to meet the boat before the sinking. When Madeleine and Marjorie got into the lifeboat they said to their father, "Come along too – there's plenty of room," and he said, "No, I'll come later." It was a case of women and children first – but there were no more lifeboats!

...People went into mourning in those days. Now new widows wear red hats or pink roses on them... That *Titanic* lifeboat went down only half full and Marjorie and a college student (man) helped row it. From the decks of the boat they saw a light on the horizon so expected to be picked up at once... I was surprised when Marjorie told me later that she gave a talk on their trip – she got information from "Father's diary". He was found floating face up, and they were given his watch and diary from his vest pocket. Mrs Newell was a fine pianist and played, really practicing, I think, into her 80s (which does not seem so astonishing to me now as I practiced mine quite a lot last summer!)'

Madeleine Crowley again:

'Mother started giving little talks on the *Titanic* in her 90s. Her greatest concern about the huge interest in the *Titanic* was that some of the money raised at conventions and so on be donated to good causes. She appeared on television a number of times and certainly enjoyed meeting up with other survivors at reunions.

After mother's death in 1992 I began looking into our family history. The death of my grandfather devastated the family for many years and I wanted to find out more about him. When I was growing up his very name – Arthur – was almost equated in my mind with heroes from myth and legend because he was so venerated in our home. That feeling of awe never really left me. Therefore, I have begun my own research to find out a bit more about the man behind the "legend".

Mother told me that after my grandmother passed away she paid a visit to Lichfield in England to see Captain Smith's memorial statue. Later she went into the cathedral there and heard some beautiful music being played. She took it as a sign – that the burden of her father's death had finally lifted and that now she could openly talk about the disaster. However, sometimes she would find it very emotional. She said, "I'll never forget the screams of the drowning. It was absolutely terrible."'

Marjorie Newell spent some of her spare time on board the *Titanic* practicing her violin. I wonder if any of the other passengers caught the strains of a few bars of Mozart or Schubert as they passed her stateroom? The door would, I suspect, have been firmly closed, as neither Marjorie nor her father approved of 'showing off' in public.

One of my favourite pieces of music is 'Beim schlafengehen' ('Falling asleep') from *Four Last Songs* by Richard Strauss. In the third song – the lyrics of which are quoted at the beginning and end of this thread – there is a 14-bar violin solo. It is a bitter-sweet, haunting melody. Romantic flights of fancy lead me to imagine a young woman playing such a tune as the *Titanic* ploughed its way through the water towards Valhalla.

'And my soul, unguarded,
Would soar free in flight,
to live deep a thousand-fold
in night's magic circle.'

LANCASTRIA
(1940)

8 November 2003

For the past few months I have been corresponding with men who survived the loss of the *Lancastria*, which sank on 17 June 1940. Reading between the lines it seems clear that many of them feel cheated that 'their' shipwreck never got the press it deserved. I can see why. Say the word 'Titanic' and every man and his dog has heard about it. 'Lancastria'? What's that? I've certainly never seen the *Lancastria* disaster featured in a movie – though it would be just as dramatic as anything you'll find in *A Night to Remember* or *Pearl Harbor*. My mind boggles when I think of the scale of it – the sheer loss of lives! Incredible.

The sinking of the *Lancastria* is the single worst maritime disaster in British history – fact. Fearing a slump in civilian wartime morale, Prime Minister Winston Churchill actually suppressed the news of the tragedy for five days, maintaining that, 'The newspapers have got quite enough disaster for today, at least.'

The disaster became a footnote in the theatre of war even though there were more people killed on the *Lancastria* than on the *Titanic* and *Lusitania* put *together*. Andrew Dixon and Ken Belsham are among the few survivors today who feel that it is a story that needs to be told. Edgar Blant lends his own perspective to the tragedy because as a young soldier he witnessed the entire event from a nearby ship.

Converted into a troop transport at the beginning of the war, the former Cunard liner *Lancastria* was requisitioned to assist in the evacuation of France, known as 'Operation Aerial', in the summer of 1940. She made her way there under the command of Captain Rudolph Sharp and anchored some 10 miles off St Nazaire on the morning of 17 June. By early afternoon she had taken on board an estimated 6,000-9,000 people, including units from the Army and RAF as well as civilians – men, women and children. It appeared that nearly every available space had been taken on the ship from deep in her massive holds right up to the boat decks. Captain Sharp feared overcrowding, but decided to wait for an escort rather than risk leaving for England without a protective convoy.

At 3.50pm the *Lancastria* was dive-bombed by five enemy planes. In the confusion and panic that followed only two lifeboats were successfully launched. Other survivors who had jumped overboard were hampered in the water by the thick black oil that oozed from the ship's ruptured fuel tanks. After twenty minutes the Lancastria turned over and sank, leaving nothing but a greasy sheen in her wake. Surrounded by the wounded and the dead, Andrew Dixon and Ken Belsham struggled for their lives, while Edgar Blant stared in disbelief at the drama unfolding before him.

Various figures for the total loss of life have been conjectured, but only 2,477 people were saved. Under the Official Secrets Act, the report on the disaster cannot be published until the year 2040. Sadly, it appears that for now, the full story of the *Lancastria* will remain hidden in her watery tomb.

ANDREW DIXON

❝ We couldn't believe it when we got on board the *Lancastria* because it was literally packed tight with troops. However, we were given a meal (our first in ten hours) and were then assigned accommodation. There were six of us altogether in our smallish cabin. It was a glorious day with the sun shining and calm waters all around. We soon settled down in our quarters and one lad produced a pack of cards and said we should while away the time by having a game or two. About half an hour later I was about to deal a hand when there was a terrific bang. The lights flickered and nearly went out. We all looked at one another in alarm. This was followed by another great blast and I said, 'I'm going up top!' We were on C deck and when I opened the cabin door there were troops dashing about all over the place trying to get upstairs.

My best mate Taff and I finally struggled to the boat deck only to find the Captain telling everyone to move from port to starboard as she was listing badly. Soon the order came to abandon ship: 'Everyone for themselves!' I turned around to say something to Taff but he wasn't there. Even though I could feel the ship going from under me I just had to find him.

I opened a steel door and stepped inside on to a small grating and I could see right down into the bowels of the ship. It was then that I spotted him. He was stretched out on a pile of cargo or something with a bottle in his hand. I could see at once that it was practically empty. He was certainly drunk. I knew that the saloon had been raided and perhaps he had panicked and helped himself. I tried my best to coax him up but it was no use. He simply wouldn't budge. What could I do? We'd been virtually inseparable since we trained together. The ship was sinking and to my horror I knew he'd be going down with it.

I went back on to the boat deck just in time to see a Nazi plane strafing the sea with his machine-guns blazing away. It was close enough for me to see the pilot so plainly that I said to myself that I would know him straight away if I ever saw his face again.

I thanked the Lord it was calm because I knew I couldn't swim well. I

Harry Slight (*right*), a third class steward, was killed on the *Titanic*, aged 34; his body was never recovered. He left a widow, Agnes, baby Winifred, Jessie and Harry (*below*). 'My mother, grandmother and I lived together in Southampton,' recalls Jessie's daughter. 'My grandmother would mention the *Titanic* often enough for it to become almost commonplace. I never gave it much thought at the time – it was just there, always in our lives.'

On 22 December 1963, on the night of the 'Tramps' Ball', a small fire broke out in the hairdressing salon of the cruise ship *Lakonia*, which quickly became a raging inferno. The Julius family survived the ensuing chaos and sinking, and were rescued by the *Salta*. Mrs Alice Julius (pointing, just to the right of the lifebelt) and her daughter Susan are seen aboard the rescue ship (*middle left*) en route to Madeira, where Susan is seen (*bottom left*), with clothes and gifts donated by local people. 'We shall always treasure all the memories of those dear people,' says Mrs Julius.

Below Like hundreds of the *Lakonia*'s passengers, Helen Gartside found no room in a lifeboat. After being in the water for three hours, she was picked up by the rescue ship *Montcalm*.

Sidney Sedunary (*above left*) was assistant to the Third Class Chief Steward on the *Titanic*. He had married on 15 October 1911, only six months before the disaster, and his son, also Sidney (*above right and right*), was born eight months after the disaster. Sidney junior has his father's wedding ring and smoking pipe, and is a real *Titanic* enthusiast with an ever-growing collection of scrapbooks on the subject.

Above Pierette Simpson was with her family migrating to the USA from Italy aboard the *Andrea Doria* when it was in collision with the Swedish liner *Stockholm* in fog on 25 July 1956. 'We lost everything, except the clothes on our back.'

Mavis Mackay (left), seen here with her sister Barbara, was with her mother on the *Duchess of Atholl* when it was torpedoed in 1942. Contemporary newspaper reports highlighted the 'calm courage and discipline' of the children, which inspired the 'hardened British seamen'.

More than 800 people were killed – including a staggering 22 entire families – when the excursion boat *Eastland* capsized on Lake Michigan in 1915. Marion Eichholz was one of only four living survivors of this American shipwreck when the author learned of her story. *Eastland Disaster Society*

Marjorie Newell was 23 years old when she survived the Titanic sinking of 1912. She lived to be 103, and retained crystal clear memories of both the ship and the disaster. However, the impression that the tragedy left on the family was so strong that it filtered through each generation, shading the lives of the women left behind.

The sinking of the *Lancastria* off St Nazaire in 1940 is the single worst maritime disaster in British history. Surrounded by the wounded and the dead, Ken Belsham (*below left*) struggled for his life in the sea, while Edgar Blant (*below right*) stared in disbelief from the deck of the nearby *Oronsay* at the drama unfolding before him.

The sinking of the *Princess Victoria* in the 'Great Storm' of January 1953 became the worst peacetime maritime disaster in British waters. National Serviceman Ivor Thomas survived when the car and passenger ferry foundered.

Right An unknown female passenger on the *Morro Castle*, unaware that 137 of the 547 people on board would perish in the imminent fire and sinking.

Below Dolly Davidson McTigue, former child star, Ziegfeld girl and model, as she was during her honeymoon cruise on the ill-fated *Morro Castle* in September 1934.

Left Barbara Anderson was the last known survivor of the *Lusitania* in the USA when the author spoke to her in 2004. 'On the day of the attack I was standing at the deck railing,' she recalled. 'Just as the torpedo struck home the Assistant Purser ... picked me up in his arms and jumped overboard into the lifeboat.'

Right Norah Wilkinson served as a VAD during the First World War and survived the sinking of the hospital ship *Britannic* as a result of enemy action off the coast of Greece on 21 November 1916.

William MacQuitty was born in Belfast on 15 May 1905, which meant that he was just past his sixth birthday when his father took him to see the *Titanic* launched on 30 May 1911. Later he produced the 1958 film version of the *Titanic* disaster – *A Night to Remember* – starring Kenneth More. He died in February 2004. *Estate of William MacQuitty*

jumped in hoping for the best. I was doing anything to keep afloat. There were bodies all over the place and I wondered how I had missed anyone when I dropped off the rope into the sea. Some of the men had been hit by debris thrown over from the soldiers on board and were injured or dead. It was pure luck if you got clear away.

I looked for a lifebelt but the only one I found was useless. It was just as well, as many of the lads who jumped overboard died because the lifebelts they had on snapped their necks as soon as they hit the water. I was literally surrounded my the living and the dead. It was pure chaos.

After about thirty minutes of bobbing about I had an experience which I shall never forget. I felt something get hold of my left leg and it was pulling me down. A thousand things flashed through my mind, then I realised that whatever it was wasn't actually hurting me. However, when I attempted to free myself I just kept sinking. Somehow my leg had found its way into the sleeve of an army greatcoat and it was stuck tight. A lad swam past me just then and I said, 'Give us a hand mate!' but he only replied, smiling, 'Sorry but I haven't got any time!' I still smile about that.

Across the water I could hear the men left on the ship singing 'Roll out the Barrel' and 'There'll always be an England'. The sea was on fire in places and it was hellish. Perhaps it was about forty minutes later when I saw a lifeboat picking up survivors. It was full and there were others swarming around it. I knew I had to try and get to it as I didn't think I could survive much longer.

After what seemed like a marathon effort I reached the boat. I managed to cling on to the safety rope for a while but soon my fingers were numb with cramp. All the while German planes continued to rain fire down on everyone in the water. Even though the *Lancastria* had sunk by then they didn't stop coming.

Suddenly a poor chap near me got hysterical. On land he would have been a straitjacket job – no question. Someone had to do something quickly. The second lieutenant had to think fast. He stood up, put his hand on his revolver and pushed his way to the mad man and shoved him into the sea. We couldn't do anything but watch.

It was shortly after this that a minesweeper came alongside and took most of us around the lifeboat on board. A sailor got hold of me and pulled me up. I must have passed out for a short while because when I came round someone had bandaged my left foot. I didn't even realise it had been injured. I was reassured that it would be taken care of when we got to the UK. We were told we would be transferred to a tramp steamer going to Plymouth.

I was taken into hospital for a short while until I was transferred to another infirmary in Basingstoke. Later on a doctor told me that he couldn't understand how they kept finding fragments in my foot and as they were non-metallic – he couldn't account for it. I told him how I had slid down the side of the *Lancastria* after letting go of a rope that someone had tied around the rails of the ship. The rope was about 15 feet too short so I had to drop the rest. The doctor laughed and said the mystery was solved. I had obviously got scale and paint flecks embedded in my foot as I slid down. I hadn't felt it at the time because I was so focused and getting away from the ship. Strange, don't you think?

KEN BELSHAM

66 Our unit was stationed at La Boule when we were told we were going home to blighty. You should have heard the cheers! We were advised to help ourselves to anything we fancied from the NAAFI so my kitbag was stuffed with eau de Cologne and chocolates. Then we set off in high spirits for the 15-mile walk to St Nazaire. Arriving at the port in darkness, we spent an uncomfortable night trying to sleep on the pavement with frequent air raids going on around us.

The following morning dawned bright and we realised there were thousands of troops all waiting to embark on two liners – the *Oronsay* and *Lancastria*. There were other boats as well, but I don't know if they were due to be used for evacuation. French tugs were plying backwards and forwards to the two ships, which were anchored a few miles away. News came through that the French had surrendered so our anxiety was even greater. We just wanted to get on board one of those ships and not get captured. There was a rumour going round that the Germans were only a few miles away.

My unit boarded the *Lancastria* at about 3pm and I managed to squeeze into a spot on the main deck. It was standing room only and very crowded! At 3.30 a bomber came over and hit the bridge of the *Oronsay*. I had a good view and saw the bridge disintegrate. A few minutes later we saw five planes in the distance – obviously positioning themselves up for a run-in to bomb us – and sure enough the *Lancastria* was hit.

Having seen the aircraft approaching I had a premonition of trouble, so I undid every button on my uniform (trousers included) and unlaced my boots. Immediately after the initial attack the ship started to list and go down by the bow on the port side. Fighter planes started machine-gunning the crowded decks – the noise was horrific – so I stripped out of my clothes. There I was with nothing on but my underpants and my identity disc. I jumped overboard and was lucky not to hit any other chaps in the water. Swimming was difficult because of this – there seemed to be hundreds of us thrashing about – and many of the soldiers were still in full kit with packs on their backs grabbing at anyone or anything in order to stay afloat. There were scenes of panic everywhere – men screaming, shouting, drowning. Every time someone lunged at me I had to dive down to get away. I'm sorry for that now but what could I do?

The *Lancastria* was plunging down and the suction was terrific. Combined with the bombs dropping everywhere around us it was like Armageddon. The ship's fuel tanks burst and the water was covered in oil, which made the going thoroughly unpleasant. A destroyer – the *Highlander*

– swept by, but it obviously couldn't stop otherwise it would have made a good bombing target, so off it went.

I turned on to my back, treading water, and to my horror I saw the mighty stern of the *Lancastria* well out of the water. There was a lifeboat dangling precariously from its falls and people were tipping out. Others were sliding down ropes – losing the skin off their hands in the process – and some were jumping off the stern and bouncing off the ship's enormous propellers like so many rubber balls. I started to pray and the Lord reassured me with the words 'My Presence shall go with you'. I was literally being sucked into the side of the ship and truly felt my life was nearing its end. But my prayers were answered. I was able to grab a rope thrown out by a sailor in a small boat, and with that I and the others were towed to a minesweeper – HMS *Cambridgeshire* – and yanked on board.

This boat was so overcrowded (I later learned that there were over 800 souls on board) that it was right down to the gunwales. Fortunately the sea was very calm. Had there been a swell we would have been doomed. However, this, for me, was the worst experience of the whole affair because we knew that the boat was a target for bombers. The boat's skipper watched out for aircraft and would take evasive action, turning the wheel this way and that. Time and time again the bombs just missed us, each explosion drenching us with water. That skipper was magnificent. He saved our lives.

The last I saw of the *Lancastria* was from the deck of HMS *Cambridgeshire* when part of the hull was covered with swarms of troops singing 'Roll out the Barrel'! One thing that I remember so clearly when swimming was the screams and cries to God. Believe me when I say there were no atheists within my hearing.

After transferring to another ship – the *John Holt* – we reached Plymouth in the early hours of Wednesday the 19th. We were welcomed by WVS ladies with tea and corned beef sandwiches. At some stage (I cannot remember when or where) I had acquired something resembling a shirt. While walking along the streets around the port, a policeman remarked to me, 'It's a good thing I'm a good copper, otherwise I'd run you in for being improperly dressed!' So you see there was still a touch of humour around. At last I got home, and a few days later my father received a telegram: 'Regretting the loss of Pte K. W. Belsham'. A chilling reminder of what might have been.

EDGAR BLANT

❝ During the war I was 1905504 Sapper E. Blant. Many years later I took holy orders and now I have a different sobriquet: Reverend Canon. However, despite my change in status I shall never forget seeing the *Lancastria* go down.

I had been stationed in France since March 1940 as part of the BEF. By June the situation had changed entirely and we were informed that we would be leaving. Thus we made our way to St Nazaire. On arrival we found ourselves at the end of a long queue along the waterside. It was 11am when I boarded a lighter and was ferried out to the *Lancastria*. When we reached the gangplank I was already standing on the gunwale with just a few men in front of me expecting to be among the first to go on board. However, an officer of the ship with a loudspeaker said, 'We are not taking any more. We are overcrowded. There is another transport expected.'

Our little craft just waited for a few hours – I know I had little sleep – until we saw the *Oronsay* arriving. As it anchored we approached it from one side while a destroyer loaded with troops stood by on the other side. We were only about two hundred yards away from the *Oronsay* when the first German bomber slipped quietly out of a cloud from just above us. It did a right wheel and bombed the bridge on the *Oronsay*. I saw four black darts falling straight on to the bridge and the whole ship was, for a moment, obscured by flame and smoke. It was 2.10pm according to my watch. The destroyer was unable to get its guns into action as it was blocked by the taller troopship. As the dust cleared I saw the naval ship pulling out from behind the *Oronsay* and it fired two shots, but by this time the plane was a mere dot on the horizon as it returned to some airfield in France that the Luftwaffe had now taken over. The pilot would have been able to report what he had seen of the evacuation going on in St Nazaire.

We went on board the *Oronsay* and I was in a fatigue party sweeping up broken glass in the first class lounge. The bridge, of course, had been demolished and I understand a lot of work had to be done to rig up fresh steering equipment. But we were not left in peace. During the afternoon relays of bombers came over and we were nearly hit again. It was utterly terrifying when a close one exploded in the sea right beside us. Occasionally a few RAF Hurricanes arrived and circled round, but their bases were in England and they could not stay long, and as they departed the next wave of bombers came at us from their bases in France. Then I heard someone say, 'They have hit the other troopship.' I went to the side and saw one end of the *Lancastria* already low in the water. It rolled over and as it sank I could see lots of black dots like flies on the upturned hull. I realised that each one was a human being.

My diary does not record the time when the *Lancastria* sank, although it does record that we finally set sail at 6pm. But during the last couple of hours small boats were transferring survivors to the *Oronsay* and some of the crew were working hard to make the ship navigable. We docked at Plymouth at 2pm on Tuesday 18 June, but only the wounded were disembarked that day and a few more survivors were taken off the next morning. The twenty or so of us who had come from Le Havre disembarked at 4pm on the Wednesday. We had spent over 48 hours on board. The feeding arrangements were very simple. I discovered a queue had formed in one of the corridors – men with mess tins at the ready. I joined the queue and eventually reached a hatch were each man received a cooked herring, a piece of bread and tea. We were marched to a park in Plymouth where we were revived with soup, which was very welcome after our adventures!

PRINCESS VICTORIA
(1953)

15 January 2004

Despite a serious and debilitating illness John McKnight happily consented to be interviewed about the *Princess Victoria*, which sank on 31 January 1953. When I interviewed him shortly after he had left hospital in January 2004, he willingly recounted his experiences of 50 years ago. I spoke to Ivor Thomas this afternoon. He was 22 years old in 1953 and was on draft from HMS *Ariel* as part of his National Service. He was taking the *Princess Victoria* over to Northern Ireland for his next posting. It is only in recent years that he has been able to bring himself to discuss the disaster, making the inclusion of his account here all the more valuable. Reading up on the last day of the *Princess Victoria* it's not hard to see why the survivors abstain from discussing the subject very often.

In January 1953 the 'Great Storm' devastated many communities in the British Isles and the near continent with great loss of life. The sinking of the *Princess Victoria*, which undertook the North Channel crossing from Larne to Stranraer, became the worst peacetime maritime disaster in British waters. It was a terrible blow to a nation still rebuilding itself after the horrors of war.

The *Princess Victoria* entered service in 1947 providing a regular passenger/car run from the west coast of Scotland to Northern Ireland. There was accommodation on board for around 1,500 passengers, with lounges and bars fitted out in a cheery, bright post-war style. Up to 40 cars could be driven over the stern and into the hold. To facilitate loading and unloading the ship was fitted with a 20-foot-diameter turntable.

The *Princess Victoria* ran into stormy weather shortly after leaving Stranraer on the morning of 31 January 1953. Her total compliment that day consisted of 179 passengers and crew. Heavy spray pounded the 5-foot-high stern door and soon water came crashing through on to the car deck. The ship took an immediate list to starboard, which was fatally increased by the 44 tons of cargo breaking their lashings and pushing the ship over on to her beam ends. An SOS was sent out by Radio Officer David Broadfoot, but soon it was all over. The *Princess Victoria* turned turtle, leaving only 44 survivors – all men – to be picked up by various rescue ships rushing to the scene.

133

David Broadfoot was posthumously awarded the George Cross for staying at his post until water filled his cabin and there was no chance of escape. More commendations followed for the crew of the RNLI and other merchant vessels that had provided rescue and support. An enquiry set up to ascertain the exact cause of the disaster highlighted the less than satisfactory stern door mechanism and put the blame squarely on the shoulders of the owners of the ship, the British Transport Commission.

JOHN MCKNIGHT

❝ Up until the *Princess Victoria* disaster nobody on the Stranraer-Larne route thought much about heavy storms. It was generally accepted in those days that service continued whatever the weather – no matter what. In fact, on the day of the storm it didn't strike me as at all unusual that we were going across – it was 'business as usual'.

As a young lad I had worked as a pantry boy and steward's boy on the ships, but when the war broke out I joined the Royal Air Force, seeing action in North Africa. When it was all over I needed a steady job so I went to the Glasgow Seaman's Cook's school to train up for the ships. I joined the LMS [London, Midland & Scottish Railway] in 1948, working on the *Princess Margaret* and *Princess Maud*, and by 1950 I was the Chief Cook on board the *Princess Victoria*. Being a new ship, she was great to work on as everything was modern. The galley was mostly stainless steel, which was easier to work with and keep clean. It was a very happy ship. Our skipper – Captain Fergusson – was very affable and well respected by the crew.

We were up and about early on the morning of 31 January as we had to prepare for the passengers arriving by train at 6am. I had to get the breakfast ready, so I didn't pay much attention to what was going on outside. By the time we sailed at 7.20am I was having to lash everything down. However, as this was not uncommon at that time of year I just got on with it and hoped that things would settle down later on. I had two assistants and a lad to help me so we just got everything in order and prepared to wait out the bad weather. By 9am we knew it wouldn't be possible to serve any more food as the rocking of the ship was too severe.

There was a considerable swell and rain lashing the ship when we left Loch Ryan and made our way into the North Channel. We had taken on a severe list and it was difficult to stand upright. Chief Officer Duckles suddenly appeared in the galley and said that things were getting 'pretty serious', and by 10am an announcement came over the Tannoy telling us to get our lifejackets on and that rescue was on its way.

As the galley was on the top deck I was able to get out with relative ease. The ship then started to heel over on to her side and I found myself scrambling up on to the side of the deck house with luggage man William Mann and Bosun William McCarlie. It was at this point that the ship started to completely capsize. I clambered over the deck rail and William

Mann gave me a leg up. I then tried to help the Bosun but he had been swept away. I now found myself standing on the keel of the ship.

I could see a lifeboat near the propeller shaft dipping up and down in the swell and I decided to make a jump for it. I landed on top of another member of the crew and knocked him out – though I was unhurt! As we moved away from the wreck we saw another lifeboat full of women and children dashed against the keel of the ship and completely destroyed. None of those poor souls were saved.

Our lifeboat had about 20 crew in it. We were washed away from the wreck and at some distance we put out the sea anchor to keep the boat into the wind. There were showers and hail blowing about us and it was terribly exposed. The last I saw of the *Princess Victoria* was her upturned hull lying low in the water.

I wasn't particularly worried about being rescued. We kept busy by bailing out the boat and pretty soon an aircraft appeared and circled round us and our spirits lifted considerably. A tanker then arrived and floated a line to us. Their crew dropped over a Jacob's Ladder for us to climb on board, but this was where my troubles began. I jumped out of the lifeboat in order to grab the ladder but the tanker's crew hadn't attached it to anything so I ended up in the water! The crew on the tanker thought I was drowning and they yelled through a megaphone to the lads in the lifeboat, 'Get him out!' They grabbed me and once more I was back where I had started. However, in the process I had lost the tops of the fingers on my right hand and had damaged my leg badly.

Eventually we were saved by a the Donaghadee lifeboat, *Sir Samuel Kelly*. Their crew called out that they would only take us one at a time to avoid a panic. They did a sterling job and gave us a bottle of rum each and a cigarette. It was very quiet on that boat; we knew that there were no women and children left. I was taken to hospital at Newton Arch and was allowed to phone my wife to tell her I was OK. I had only just got married a few days before so she was very pleased to hear from me.

The disaster didn't affect me too badly, though. Later I was happy enough to go and work for the company again and over the years I got promoted and ended up as the Purser on the *Caledonian Princess*, which did the same run as the *Princess Victoria*. Looking back on it now I wouldn't change anything in my life. Sometimes you have to go through the bad things to show you what kind of stuff you're made of.

IVOR THOMAS

❝ The ship left Stranraer at dawn; the sea was rather rough and the wind blowing a gale. I was in the lounge trying to sleep, but the roll of the ship made this difficult so I had to be content just to sit and rest.

When the ship reached the mouth of Loch Ryan and turned into the open sea it was struck by a tremendous wave, which shook the ship from stem to stern, damaging the doors of the car deck. Nobody knew of this, as nearly everyone was in the lounge, but it became rather evident that something was amiss when the ship developed a slight list to starboard. Gradually this increased until walking became very difficult. I went out on to the port gangway and walked to the stern to see the car deck doors swinging to and fro as the sea rushed in and out with every pitch of the ship.

I returned to the lounge. Half an hour later the order came over the loudspeaker: the situation was serious and lifebelts would be issued. The lifebelts were thrown from man to man along the gangway until everybody in the lounge had one. The ship was at such an angle that the people in the lounge could not climb out. By smashing the lounge windows and lowering the ropes, the remaining passengers were brought out on to the port gangway. Time passed and the position became desperate with no sign of help.

Later, as she turned on her side, the order came to abandon ship. I helped a young woman up to the boat deck and was assisting another when a wave smashed along the gangway and knocked me off my feet. I snatched at a stanchion, climbed up to the boat deck, but the whole superstructure was under water. I dived in and swam for a lifeboat. Battered by the sea, and being swept back towards the sinking hull, I caught hold of one of the trailing ropes and tried to climb in, but the sea beat me down until I could do no more than hang on. The lifeboat was swept against the hull and I was caught between them. I held my breath every time the lifeboat plunged under the water and hung on for grim death. My trousers had come loose so I kicked them off as they were hindering my efforts to get into the boat. Suddenly the lifeboat started to drift away from the hull; I waved my hand, and the occupants helped to pull me aboard. I lay in the bottom of the lifeboat recovering my breath when the shout went up, 'There she goes!' I looked to see the ship hover for a minute out of the water and then make its last dive.

The lifeboat was taking water as each wave smashed over us and we had to bail it out as best we could. We continued drifting on our sea anchor for a considerable time until a ship was sighted off the port bow. It moved away as if it had not sighted us, but a few minutes later altered course. We drifted under the stern, which was smashing violently against our bow, and it was evident that unless the tanker moved away we would be smashed. The Captain of the tanker heard our cries, pulled her away and stood by in case the lifeboat should founder. The destroyer *Contest* was also near at hand, but the most heart-warming sight of all was when the Donaghadee lifeboat appeared. It seemed to leap from crest to crest and was alongside us before we could realise that we were saved.

Jumping across the railings was no difficulty and we were soon below, smoking and recovering fast with the help of a tot of rum. The lifeboat cruised around looking for other survivors, then set course for Donaghadee. Tired and exhausted as we were, we still managed to raise a little smile as we walked along the quay to the waiting ambulances, which took us to Bangor Hospital.

Titanic threads...
Titanic and a Tommy

September 2004: since the beginning of term I've been reading a book with one of my lower school classes called *Private Peaceful* by Michael Morpurgo. It's about a teenager who enlists with his brother in the First World War. I think it's a marvellous book, but I was unprepared for the enthusiasm of the students. It's got to the point that if we don't read it in class for whatever reason they get resentful. Today was such a day.

'When are we going to read *Private Peaceful* again?' one boy said to me with a hurt expression.

We had ten minutes left, so I said, 'Would you like to hear about how I met a *real* Tommy?'

Their usual teenage studied indifference changed to mild interest – just. It was a 'Show me!' moment, the kind that every teacher dreads.

I recounted how I had met a First World War veteran called Albert 'Smiler' Marshall back in 2000. I'd always wanted to meet someone who had actually been there, in the trenches, to ask them what it was like. Smiler (as he insisted on being called) was 102 years old when I met him – general amazement from the class that anyone could live that long – and he told me all about how he had put up his age to join up (he was just seventeen), how to avoid trench foot ('I used to rub my rum ration on my feet to stop it'), and how he coped with the lice. In all, Smiler was involved with the fighting from Christmas 1914 right up until the bitter end in 1918 – not unlike the very 'Private Peaceful' we had been reading about.

The bit they loved the most, however, was when I told them about Smiler's confusion over my age. His sight was not good and after relating most of his story we got on to the Second World War. By that time Smiler was middle-aged of course. There was a pause. He then turned to me and said, 'What did you do in the last war?' A trifle bemused I replied that I was too young to remember it. He seemed satisfied with that and sat back. On that day in February 2000 I was 27. It didn't surprise the students though. To them, any teacher appears to be between the age of grown-up and death! The bell went then and the students shuffled off.

Naturally enough, when I spoke to Smiler the focus of our conversation was the First World War. But the *Titanic* made an appearance all the same. It happened when I asked him how he kept his spirits up in the trenches:

'The parson would come right up to us before we went to the front line and say, "However near you are to death, there's somebody nearer." That helped a bit. If I fell down today I wouldn't get up until I sang *Nearer My God To Thee*. My Sunday school teacher went down on the *Titanic* and it used to give me comfort to know that he was one of those leading the prayers as the ship went down. They sang *Nearer My God To Thee*.'

I never did ascertain whether Smiler's teacher really did end up on the *Titanic*. It doesn't matter. In my eyes he's a true hero – and besides, it makes a good story even better.

MORRO CASTLE
(1934)

12 September 2004

The story of the last days of the *Morro Castle* is worthy of a plot in an Agatha Christie novel! There is a palpable air of mystery about the whole event. Today I chatted at some length to a lady who managed to survive the *Morro Castle* when it caught fire at sea on 8 September 1934. Dolly Davidson McTigue, a former child star, Ziegfeld girl and model, told me that it was like landing herself a featured part in a watery drama that she could have well done without!

However, to stay with a theatrical theme for a moment, consider this story about the curious knock-on effect of the disaster.

In September 1934 an exciting new musical with music and lyrics by Cole Porter was about to begin rehearsals on Broadway. Ethel Merman and William Gaxton were to star and the action was to take place on board a liner that gets shipwrecked. Originally called *Bon Voyage*, then *Hard to Get*, rehearsals ground to a halt when news of a terrible real-life shipwreck reached Manhattan. Clearly the libretto would have to be hurriedly changed. Howard Lindsay and Russel Grouse undertook emergency re-writes, and though the show would still take place on board a ship, there would be no need for the cast to 'take to the lifeboats'. In desperation the show was renamed *Anything Goes*, and was a smash. The ship that inadvertently helped to shape that Broadway hit was, of course, the *Morro Castle*.

Commissioned by the Ward Line and intended for the New York-Cuba run, the *Morro Castle* was a two-funnelled liner, 531 feet in length and capable of 20 knots. With a cornucopia of interior design schemes it was comfortable rather than chic, but throughout its four-year service history it remained popular with the general public.

The *Morro Castle* was on its return leg from Havana when at 2.45am on the morning of 8 September 1934 a small fire was detected in the First Class Writing Room. Faulty fire-fighting equipment and a crew unprepared for such an emergency ensured that the *Morro Castle* was quickly enveloped in smoke and flames. An SOS was dispatched nearly half an hour after the fire had been initially detected, but it was too little too late. Six miles off the Jersey coast, passengers and crew dropped into the heaving swell – many to die of exposure and burns. Of the 547 people on board a total of 137 were killed.

The smouldering wreck drifted on the tide until it came to rest on a sand bank at the seaside resort of Asbury Park, New Jersey. It soon became a macabre tourist attraction with an audience of thousands until it was wrested from the sand and towed away for scrap some weeks later.

An enquiry was established in an attempt to try to answer the myriad of questions surrounding the disaster. What had caused Captain Wilmott's death the day *before* the fire? Why had an SOS not been sent earlier? Could it be proven conclusively that there were pro-Communist agitators aboard? If so, was the fire an act of arson or simply an unfortunate accident? Why had there been no fire drill for passengers or crew? Why were eight of the lifeboats unlaunchable? What possessed acting Captain Warms to turn the *Morro Castle* into the 40mph wind and in doing so fan the flames? Had some of the crew abandoned their posts and saved themselves first? None of these questions were ever satisfactorily explained, and today the *Morro Castle* disaster is arguably one of the strangest and most mysterious in maritime history.

The bad publicity marked a downward turn in business for the Ward Line. A year later the *Morro Castle*'s replacement ship, *Mohawk*, ran across the bow of a freighter and sank within sight of the *Morro Castle* fire with a loss of 40 lives – most of whom froze to death in their lifeboats. The ensuing scandal was one of the major factors in the Ward Line changing its name to the Cuba Mail Line.

DOLLY DAVIDSON MCTIGUE

" In those days Cuba was an exciting and exotic destination so my husband Sydney and I decided to take a honeymoon cruise aboard the *Morro Castle* because the ship was so beautiful and the length of the cruise was just right. We hoped it would be a romantic start to our married life.

I had been a child actress both on screen and stage and by quite an early age I had appeared with the legends Katherine Cornell and W. C. Fields. At the time of the *Morro Castle* trip I was 21 years old and working as a model on 5th Avenue, New York. My husband was the owner of a fabric business, selling to the fashion houses. Being reasonably comfortable we decided to splash out and go first class.

The night before we were to dock in Havana I fell over on the boat deck and sprained my ankle. Sydney and I therefore stayed on board instead of exploring the city. It wasn't so bad though, as Sydney surprised me with a wedding gift of a fur coat and a diamond watch. These and all our other possessions were lost during the tragedy that followed.

Our cabin was pleasant enough, but some of the staterooms were quite enchanting. I particularly recall the first class lounge and dining room as being quite exquisite. The service on board was attentive and the food was very good indeed. In all, we were more than happy – being newly married adding to our general good spirits, I suppose!

We didn't have a lifeboat or fire drill once while we were aboard. We did see a hose turned on at one point, very briefly, but I noticed that there were holes in it and practically no water pressure – only a trickle of water coming through. Actually it was rather funny. No one seemed bothered about it though, and we didn't give it much thought – not then at least.

There was quite a bit of drinking and partying going on. Everyone was very sociable and determined to have a good time. The ship's orchestra piped out lovely tunes, which we danced to every night.

For the last night of the cruise we were invited to attend the gala dinner at the Captain's table. Naturally, we were both very excited and looking forward to it tremendously. Suddenly word was sent out that Captain Wilmott had died of a heart attack and that all subsequent festivities were to be cancelled. A sort of gloom spread over everyone after that. Some passengers were suspicious because the Captain had appeared to be in such good health just a few hours before. So Sydney and I had a quiet dinner followed by a nightcap and went to bed early.

At about 3.00am, Sydney was awakened by a noise in the hall. He opened the door and people were running up and down calling out, 'Fire! Fire! – the ship's on fire!' Sydney threw on his trousers and buttoned his coat around me and we went out with the other passengers. One of the crew – who I recognised as our Cruise Director, Mr Smith – led a group of us to one end of the ship, but there was simply too much smoke and fire to proceed any further. Back we trooped to the other end, but we were driven back by the intense heat. So the only way was up a stairwell to a higher deck. Wherever we went the fire turned us back. It was total bedlam with people running and screaming – heat, smoke and flames all over the place. By now passengers were shouting out, 'Where are the lifeboats?' but we hadn't seen any being made ready – though incredibly there already appeared to be some bobbing about in the water below. Oddly, some of them seemed to contain more crew than passengers.

People began jumping in the water. Sydney had managed to find two lifejackets from our stateroom and he now fastened one on me and put on his own. A young child asked us for a lifejacket and Sydney gave his to him. He then went searching for another one because he knew that he would never survive in the water without it. I saw none of the crew other than the Mr Smith who told us that the rest of them had disappeared. There was total panic and people were pushing and shoving in order to get off the ship before they were burned alive. I was both numb and scared out of my wits. Finally, in desperation, Sydney told me that we had to jump for our lives, but the thought of it terrified me. It was so far down to the ocean from the deck and the waves were so high. Sydney jumped and as I looked overboard another passenger grabbed hold of my feet and just tipped me over the rail. Amazingly, I landed right next to my husband.

We were in the water more than seven hours. To keep our spirits up we joined hands with other passengers in a circle. Sometimes we sang songs and sometimes we just prayed. We had to keep our feet moving because the lifejackets were the old 'Mae West' type. We tried to hold a young child up, passing him along from one of us to another, but finally he was just taken from us in a huge wave. By then he was already dead.

It was simply terrible seeing dozens of burnt corpses floating by. People called out that there were sharks, which didn't help! Twice I tried to swim to a lifeboat but was either turned away by people who said it was too full or the size of the waves further deterred my efforts. The older people didn't stand a chance in that water. They just disappeared or drowned. I remember seeing this girl in the water with long black hair. She was completely burnt. It was a dreadful sight, but in a strange way it gave me hope. I just became more determined to live. I kept repeating to myself, 'I won't die! I won't!'

When it got light we saw another lifeboat between the waves and Sydney said that we had to try and make it. We couldn't survive any longer in the water. When we got to the boat the people said again, 'No, no, too full!' but Sydney pushed me up and then climbed aboard himself; in doing so, he broke all the fingers on one of his hands.

It was daylight by now when a big ship appeared and they threw a rope down to us and we were hoisted aboard. We were taken to the boiler room to dry off and generally we were treated very well. We were told that the Captain wanted to see us – were Mr and Mrs Sydney Davidson on board? He took us to his cabin and gave us a drink and a newspaper 'off the record'. We couldn't think why we were singled out like that and I still don't know to this day. On reaching shore, we were put into a limousine and taken to a hotel where a doctor checked us over. I thought that was rather special treatment! Had news got round that we were on our honeymoon? A few reporters turned up and wanted to know all about our ordeal, and subsequently we found ourselves in the *Daily Mirror* next day under the headline 'Escaped Horrible Death Aboard Liner'. We also received a $200 settlement for our troubles from the Ward Line.

I credit my survival to a plain determination to live, a refusal to think of myself as 'lost at sea' and lying in a casket – plus a lot of praying and faith. Ever since the *Morro Castle* disaster I have not set foot on another ship and cannot watch movies about disasters at sea. In fact, just looking at the ocean from the beach makes me feel a little odd even today. It just brings it all back.

Sydney and I returned to New York and soon after we had our first child – a boy. I was diagnosed with tuberculosis, which the doctors thought was a result of the long exposure I had undergone in the water. I was sent to a sanatorium in upstate New York for a lengthy stay. Sadly, although Sydney and I had endured so much already we were not able to survive the long separation and eventually we divorced. I returned to the fashion industry, remarried, had another boy and was widowed. I continued to work until my retirement at 65.

I have been to a number of reunions but although I found them interesting I, and the other survivors, did not generally like discussing our experiences in any detail. I still get bad dreams about it and it feels too sad thinking about picturing the dead floating around me in the sea – it was horrible, just horrible. So many people died because of plain negligence and poor organisation. The whole affair is still such a mystery, isn't it? No one really knows why that fire started, do they? It's a story full of intrigue and not something I feel ever likely to forget.

23 November 2003

The sad tale of the *Morro Castle* continues. A Mr Robert Lione has written to me from Yonkers, New York, with some information about the effect the disaster had on his family.

ROBERT LIONE

❝ My late father, Anthony Lione, was named 'Salesman of the Year' by his employer. The cruise on the *Morro Castle* was his award! We took the cruise also to celebrate my parents' 10th wedding anniversary.

I remember little of the disaster as I was only four years and ten months old at the time. I do know that my father and brother jumped overboard. They were excellent swimmers and would probably have made it if others had not clung to them. My mother did not wish to jump so stayed on board. Ultimately a member of the crew tied a rope around me and lowered me over the side. I do remember dangling in the cold water. My mother slid down a rope and suffered serious burns, which required a lengthy hospitalisation. We were both picked up by lifeboats from another ship, the *Monarch of Bermuda*, which was about 30 miles away at the time of the disaster. We were returned to the New York pier on that ship.

[Mr Lione also enclosed this clipping, which 'fleshes out' his account:]

DEATH TAKES HALF OF FAMILY

Ship Fire Victims' Coffins Tragic Anniversary Finale

Two flower-bedecked coffins side by side in the living room of their home Sunnyside in Queens yesterday were the mute finale to a joyous wedding anniversary celebration that ended in the flaming ruins of the *Morro Castle*. For ten years, Anthony and Mary Lione had worked hard to maintain their home and bring up two husky boys. They decided to take a vacation: they and the children, Raymond, 9, and Bobby, 4.

Mother, One Son Return

Two of them came back from that trip – Bobby, who still prattles innocently at the home of a relative, unmindful of the tragedy, and the mother, suffering the pains of a flame-seared body in Flower Hospital and the deeper anguish of her double loss. Her husband and other son will be buried tomorrow.

Mrs Lione's story vividly caught the horror of it all.

'We rose hastily at the sounds of alarm,' she said. 'I did not stop to dress, but clothed the two boys. The boats had been lowered; we were on the deck about an hour and a half. Then I saw my husband and Raymond lowered over the side. They let Bobby down next and I lost sight of him until we were carried aboard the *Monarch of Bermuda*.'

The last the mother heard of any of them was the voice of Raymond crying as he was let over the side.

'They've got to save me! I don't want to die!'

Body Taken Ashore

But his body was one of those taken ashore at Sea Girt. He was to have entered school yesterday as a fourth grade student.

His father, Anthony, 34, a year older than his wife, was a salesman in the Jamaica office of an insurance company. He had been an architect, and previous to that, an orchestra leader.

The two will be buried in Calvary Cemetery tomorrow, following a requiem mass in St Teresa's Catholic Church, where Lione was an usher.

Meanwhile, the bodies lie together at home, lights from candles in front of the crucifixes flickering on the faces of the father and of Raymond, the boy who did not want to die.

Titanic threads...
Ron Kroepfl

'In that grandest nation I'll stand tall
Reach my very highest hopes of all...
Better place for me and you...
Better land to start anew...'
Titanic, a musical, Maury Yeston

As a boy Ron Kroepfl adored visiting his Aunt Louise. In the 1950s, before creeping urbanisation overwhelmed the district, her small farm in Wisconsin was an idyllic place where an energetic lad like him could run around, climb trees, go off exploring through the nearby valley, and come back tired but happy, ready for some of his Aunt's delicious home cooking.

'She always made me something nice,' recalls Ron today, 'like home-preserved berry jam or tangy pickles. She was a dear.'

He soon found out that she was a pretty special person in other ways too. In the best parlour little Ron had often observed the old, brown cardboard photographs mounted on the wall above the fireplace.

'They were hard to miss because they were so large!' he laughs. Who were those funny-looking people, he wondered. Why were the photographs so important to Aunt Louise? One day, filled with curiosity, he asked her.

'"Those photographs were taken in 1912," she said. "It was just after my parents and I had arrived in America." She continued by saying how very happy and relieved they were to get here. I asked her why. "Well, because we came on the *Titanic*." Now *that* got me very interested indeed! "I was only a little girl at the time," she explained, "so I don't remember that much about it, only what my mother told me later on. Do you still want to hear it?"

I *begged* her to tell me what she knew. Young boys have the subtlety of a sledgehammer and it never even occurred to me that it might be in any way painful for her to talk about it so I just blundered on. But then she was very sweet (not to mention patient) and told me the whole thing.

The story goes that the family was emigrating to Milwaukee from Switzerland. There was my grandmother (also called Louise), my grandfather Anton, and Aunt Louise, who was four years old. Anton's younger brother Vincenz and his sister Maria were also emigrating, so it was quite a family gathering. They were hoping to become farmers, and since money was so tight they were all going steerage.

After boarding the *Titanic* at Southampton the men and the women were separated and directed to berths at opposite ends of the ship. On that fatal night Anton said he actually felt the collision with the iceberg in his cabin and went out to see what had happened. Legend has it that he even saw it gliding by, a large black mass floating off into the distance. Anton knew instinctively that it was serious so he ran helter-skelter down the stairs, back to his cabin and promptly packed his belongings. He couldn't afford to lose anything because that was all the family had in the world. By the time he was finished there was water sloshing around his feet. Desperate now to find his wife and child he rushed from one end of the *Titanic* to the other, fighting his way past the other passengers. It was terrifying because he hardly spoke any English and the crew were shouting orders and he couldn't make sense of it. But he understood enough to know that there was something very wrong with the ship because he could feel it listing towards the bow. Even *he* knew that wasn't right!

Thankfully he found both his Louises, but in all the confusion Vincenz and Maria got lost. There was so little time and he knew he had to get the two of them safely up to the boat deck. Somehow they ended up in the first class, which was quite a sight! But there was no time to stop and gaze at their surroundings. Spotting an exit they pitched up on to the boat deck and went in search of a lifeboat. Louise and her mother were put into lifeboat 2 but the men were asked to stay behind. Well, poor Anton had done so much to get them this far, so he was heartbroken. But despite loud protestations from both mother and daughter the boat started its squeaky descent. With nothing to lose, Anton took a jump and landed in the boat as it was going down to the water. He was determined to make sure his family got to America no matter what and he couldn't let them go alone without him.

The whole affair left four-year-old Louise cold with terror. After that night she couldn't remember a single thing about it. It was almost as if the *Titanic* had never happened because she retained a total amnesia about the ship, brought on by shock, which lasted her whole life.

My grandmother told me that her hair turned completely white after the disaster – despite being only 26 at the time – and that's the only thing she ever said to me about it. Of course, when I knew her she was a very old lady, so I can't verify that. Basically, her lips were sealed as far as the *Titanic* was concerned. However, it was clear that the disaster had affected her in other ways as time went on.

Grandmother was a very reserved person and would only talk German. When I was young I was told not to mention the *Titanic* disaster in her company. The whole subject was a non-starter, which was sad because she knew so much and I would have loved asking her about it. It was like a shadow hanging over the family. So I had to turn to Aunt Louise for more details when we were alone together. Grandmother was not, I think, the easiest person to live with, and my grandfather Anton and she separated in 1919. He went off to South America and remarried, which was sad for Aunt Louise because she never saw her father again and she used to often tell me what a lovely, kind man he was. Thinking about it now, the *Titanic* may have saved their lives but it put too much strain on their marriage. So they were casualties of the disaster in a different way.

For all the difficulties in their relationship, Aunt Louise looked after her mother until the day she died. Grandmother could be a demanding woman and I don't think it was easy for my aunt in any way, but she never once complained. Family always came first and that was that.

Her life had been pretty hard, though; farming is not an easy job. But she had a natural gift for working the land – real green fingers. Her fruit and vegetables were amazing – huge! I don't know if she entered any competitions but she certainly should have! She never sat still, was always on the go, up and doing. Right up until the end she was like that. People had to run to keep up with her even though she was absolutely tiny.

I believe it was only after my grandmother passed away in 1979 that my aunt felt she could discuss the disaster more openly and freely. You see, she was a small lady with a big heart. She had four children of her own and after they grew up she wanted to give something back to society. The *Titanic* was a way for her to do that because she was asked to do interviews and so forth for historical research. She absolutely loved getting involved with *Titanic*-related events and wouldn't hesitate to sign autographs for people. She adored children especially, and couldn't resist them if they wanted 'just one more photo'. And by the late 1980s she was unstoppable!

When she was very old Aunt Louise was asked to go on the *QE2* to place some headstones on the graves of some of the *Titanic* victims who had recently been identified. She agreed to do it straight away because she knew that she was one of the few survivors left who could physically undertake the journey. She loved America and being an American, and she wanted so much to help honour those who never made it here.'

Louise Kink died in August 1992. During our interview Ron said, 'It fills me with pride to know that Aunt Louise trusted me at such a young age to tell me all about how she was saved from the *Titanic*. Having a grown-up family of my own, and grandchildren, it's a wonderful story to pass down to the next generation. How many people can say they have something like the *Titanic* in their family history? Her life after the *Titanic* was tough, but at least the family came through that calamity together where so many others had their lives destroyed.'

BRITANNIC
(1916)

10 March 2005

'**M**y mother didn't talk about the First World War much at all,' said George Cooke during our interview. 'You see, she was a very reserved woman and didn't want to revisit those times. As a clergyman's wife, she devoted her energies to good works such as the Mothers Union and the British Red Cross. I suppose she was a woman typical of her age; duty and charity were the guiding principles of her life.'

George Cooke had an idea that his mother, Norah Wilkinson, had served as a VAD during the First World War and had once been on a huge ship that sank. But he had never been able to glean much more information than that during her life. It was as if the gates to Norah's past had been locked and bolted. After her death in the early 'sixties, he began to put the missing pieces together for himself. Starting with a sheaf of papers and correspondence he was finally able to shed some light on his mother's wartime adventures.

'My mother was on the *Britannic* when she sank on 21 November 1916,' he told me. 'After launching in 1914, the 47,500-ton, four-funnel White Star *Britannic* was sister ship of the *Titanic*, was brought into immediate use as a hospital ship, but was sunk as a result of enemy action off the coast of Greece. My mother was picked up from a lifeboat at 10.30am to go on board the ship *Scourge* and was subsequently transferred to the *Duncan*, which arrived at Piraeus at 5.30pm. After a week in Athens she left on the small hospital ship *Grand Tully* and arrived in Malta on 1 December 1916 before returning to Southampton on the hospital ship *Valdivea*.

'When the *Britannic* sank, 28 people were drowned, but fortunately the wounded soldiers who were due to be taken back to England had not been picked up and the rest of the crew and nursing staff, totalling about 1,000, managed to get to other ships and eventually to shore. In a short letter dated 23 November 1916, on paper headed Aktaion, Phalere, Greece, my mother wrote to her mother.'

The letter read:

'Here I am quite safe and well after our awful experiences. You can imagine we are very lucky to be alive at all. None of the nurses were hurt but some of the crew and RAMC very badly injured and others dead. We do not know when we leave of where we shall go to. I may get home before this but will let you know as soon as ever I can. We have lost all, only got what we stand up in! People are awfully good here to us. Best love to all. In haste to catch the mail.'

On 1 December 1916 George's mother wrote at greater length to her mother from St Andrew's Military Hospital in Malta. It is interesting that this letter included the following comment:

'I wish they would send us to Egypt but I do not want to go on another ship till the war is over. The people in Athens were awfully kind to us and wept when we came away. I was awfully lucky, I went to the Russian Hospital and helped. I said I could talk a little French so I got there and had to interpret for the Sisters! What! What!'

As a student at University I enjoyed reading Vera Brittain's autobiography *Testament of Youth*. Brittain was, like Norah Wilkinson, a VAD and also travelled on board the *Britannic* before it sank. Her first impressions of the ship were mixed:

'When we came near to the Isle of Wight, the *Britannic*, anchored off Cowes, appeared in the distance like a huge white mammoth lying on its side. For a moment a sick dread had seized me when I learned that she had been built as sister ship to the *Titanic*, but as I watched her scarlet crosses and four large funnels gleaming in the low sunshine, I consoled myself by reflecting that her conversion into a hospital ship had removed her to a different category.'

Despite the on-board restrictions imposed by imperious Matrons and the stark appearance of the ship – stripped of most of her luxurious fittings – Brittain made the best of it and settled down quickly. The *Britannic* reached Mudros harbour without incident. However, the ship and the inherent dangers of passing through enemy-infested waters had left a strong impression on the author:

'Six months afterwards, writing to my mother about the torpedoing of the *Asturia* with two of our most popular Malta VADs on board, I tried to describe the disintegrating fear which left me with a sick reluctance to undertake long voyages that ignominiously persists to this day.

I feel so sorry for them to think it happened at night, for I remember

the feelings of terror the dark hours used to bring us on *Britannic* –
feelings which, of course, we never mentioned to each other at the time
but afterwards all admitted we had. I used to look over the steep side
of that tremendous ship and think to myself: "Perhaps now – or now
– or now!" It is being on the qui vive for something that may happen
any moment of any hour which makes the strain of a long voyage
nowadays. "Betty" and I were not in a very good place for being
torpedoed on the *Britannic* as having a cabin we were on a lower deck
than most of the others – in fact we were only a yard or two from the
place where the torpedo ultimately went through. I used to wake up at
night and listen to the thrash of the screws and the whistle of the wind
above the mastheads and the rushing of the water against the side, and
wonder if any among the strange occasional crashes and bangs that
went on all night was a torpedo or mine striking the ship.'

Later, after the *Britannic* had sunk (by a mine or torpedo, nobody is quite
sure), Vera Brittain went to see a Sister whom she had met on a previous
voyage. She found her quite altered by her experiences on the sinking
Britannic. I wonder if Norah Wilkinson felt the same way?

'[She was] nervous, distressed and all the time on the verge of crying.
But to talk of the disaster seemed to bring her relief, and from her
conversation we learnt the story of the ship's last hours.

The explosion, she told us, occurred during breakfast: it blew up the
bottom of the main staircase, together with an orderly who happened
to be there at the time. The nursing staff marched quietly out of the
dining saloon; they were told to fetch any valuables that they could get
quickly and reassemble at once on the boat deck. The "valuables"
taken illustrated the strange workings of a mind trying to control its
own panic; one girl seized her fountain pen and left £30 in notes under
the pillow.

The old Matron, motionless as a rock, sat on the boat deck and
counted the sisters and nurses as they file past her into the boats,
refusing to leave until all were assembled. None of the women were
lost; but a number of the casualties occurred among the orderlies
through the smashing of the last two boats by the propeller as the ship
lurched over on her side. The medical officers, remaining to the end,
climbed down the wire ropes – which almost cut their hands to pieces
– dropped into the sea in their lifebelts, and struggled to the boats
already afloat. Two of them disappeared and were never accounted for.

In one of the boats sat the Matron, looking towards the doomed
Britannic while the rest of its occupants, with our friend amongst
them, anxiously scanned the empty horizon. She saw the propeller cut
a boat in half and fling its mutilated victims into the air, but, for the
sake of the young women for whom she was responsible, she never
uttered a sound nor moved a muscle of her grim old face. What a pity

it is, I meditated as I listened ... that outstanding heroism seems so often to be associated with such unmitigated limitations! How seldom it is that this type of courage goes with an imaginative head, a sensitive, intelligent mind!

They spent three hours in the boats, concluded the Sister, before they saw two rescue destroyers racing over the edge of the calm, sunny sea. Among those saved was a stewardess who had been on the *Titanic*... At first their rescuers had looked, not for the boats, but for the *Britannic* herself, never dreaming, in spite of the fate of the *Lusitania*, that so great a ship could have gone down so soon.

Actually she sank in three-quarters of an hour, and for many of the survivors, already sick with shock, the worst part of their ordeal was the sight of her disappearance. Incredulously horrified, they watched porthole after porthole slide under the water, until at length she heeled right over and went down in a pitiless whirlpool. The dreadful cry of the last siren, "All hands off the ship!" just before she sank would haunt their nights, our friend said, for the rest of their lives.'

LUSITANIA
(PART 2)

20 March 2004

A researcher friend of mine in America rang me this morning to inform me that I should really talk to a woman called Barbara Anderson if I was going to include the *Lusitania* in this collection. I'd never heard of her.

'Who is she?' I enquired.

'The last known *Lusitania* survivor over here. Didn't you know?'

I was surprised and delighted as I genuinely thought that, apart from Audrey Pearl, all of the survivors had died.

'Have you got her number?' I asked.

He told me that she was a personal friend and that she would enjoy hearing from me. Today, therefore, I had a long chat with one of the only other *Lusitania* survivors in the world. Barbara appeared to be pleased to talk at length about that day way back in 1915. Unlike Audrey Pearl, who was a babe in arms, Barbara could actually remember something of the ship and was more than happy to answer my questions. She finished by inviting me over to her next summer barbeque! It never ceases to amaze me how generous total strangers are with me – not only with their time but in extending the hand of friendship.

BARBARA ANDERSON

❝ I was on the *Lusitania* when she was torpedoed because my mother wanted to go back home to England to see her parents. My father had emigrated to America a few years before my mother, and then when he got settled he sent for her to come over. They were married there and I was born in Connecticut in June 1912. We left for England on the Lusitania in May 1915. Mother and I were booked into second class. The day before we left, my father took us both to Bridgeport to say goodbye to all our friends. I was suitably dressed in a sailor suit.

On the day of the attack I was standing at the deck railing. Just as the torpedo struck home the Assistant Purser, Mr Harkness, saw me. He picked me up in his arms and jumped overboard into the lifeboat. I wasn't injured or anything – even though I was taken to hospital later for a check-up. My poor mother had to jump into the sea but luckily she was rescued a little later. Apart from that, the only thing I can remember of the *Lusitania* itself before the disaster is the charming dining saloon. I was told later that for a while we were listed as 'lost – presumed dead'.

The next thing I recall was being in Liverpool and seeing my Aunt Edith waiting anxiously for us on the station platform – relieved to see us safe and well. Strangely enough, after we were rescued I was found to be still holding a spoon that I must have picked up from the dining saloon or somewhere. For some reason I had clutched hold of it and in the panic and excitement I never let it go. My Granny kept it safe in a drawer and would show it to visitors rather like a medal.

In 1919 I travelled on the *Lusitania*'s sister ship, *Mauritania*, back to my father. It cost 15 pounds and 12 shillings. My Aunt Annie wanted to keep me in England but in the end I had to go. Although I was only seven years old I can remember the captain who was terribly kind. He even asked me if I wanted to be his dinner companion one evening! Naturally I said yes straightaway. That was Captain Arthur Rostron who, in 1912, had rescued all the *Titanic* survivors in the *Carpathia*. I was delighted!

Being so young at the time, the *Lusitania* disaster did not effect me greatly as an adult. However, it took me quite a while to get people to listen to me and know I was telling the truth about it! People used to find it incredible that I had been on the *Lusitania*, though heaven knows why! The family never talked about it much and I have not met any other survivors. I believe that the truth about the disaster is finally surfacing. So many people seem to be interested in it and many times I have been delighted to get letters from people giving me information about the ship and the disaster. However, I did not care to hear that there have been items raised from the wreck – very poor taste indeed. There has been a lot of fuss about the *Titanic* but really the *Lusitania* was just as bad.

Later on I married and have a son who is now 65 and a daughter who is 60. I have two grandsons and three great-grandsons. I have not taken a ship to England since the late 1910s although I did go back in 1974 by plane. I visited my Granny's house and saw my dear Aunt Annie – my dad's sister. They are all gone now. People always think I look much younger than I am and they are shocked when they meet me! They say I don't look that old. But they're always interested when I tell them about the *Lusitania*. Who can blame them?

2 April 2004

Another titbit in the post today from my American colleague about Barbara's experiences on the *Lusitania*. This time a clipping from a local newspaper, the *North Star* – dated 1915 – which sheds even more light on how the Andersons survived:

'Darlington Lady Survivor From the Lusitania
A Graphic Statement

Mrs Roland Anderson, who, with her little daughter are among the survivors of the *Lusitania*, was seen last evening at Darlington by a *North Star* representative. Her husband is a draughtsman at Bridgeport, in the State of Connecticut. She left England some five years ago and is now staying with her parents, who, by the way, have a son fighting for his country as a despatch rider at the front.

Mrs Anderson looks none the worse for her terrible experience, and her charming little daughter was prattling away merrily with the innocence of childhood.

Mrs Anderson said they had had a charming passage. The weather was fine all the way, and few, if any, of the passengers regarded the submarine threats as really dangerous. When they left New York there were many warships about, and they anticipated seeing many more when approaching England, but saw none. Friday was a glorious day, and it was about luncheon time that the torpedo, the first presumably, struck the liner. She heaved over with a terrible list in moments. 'I was in the saloon at the time,' said Mrs Anderson, 'and I made for the boat deck at once. Some one carried my little daughter up the stairs to the deck, or I might not have got there. The deck was at such an angle that we slid down towards the boats. I got into one with its covers on, but I was ordered into another one which was ready.'

There was no panic and the rule Women and Children First was carried out. There was no need to lower the boats, for they were touching the water. They simply cut away the ropes from the davits.

They were so near the sides of the liner that they thought they would go down with the suction, but the men got the oars out quickly and managed to keep clear. The liner went under, as a matter of fact, quite smoothly. They were afraid, too, of the funnels, which seemed to be coming right upon then. One lady got so frightened that she jumped into a funnel to be swept out again and to be picked up again.

After a while they came across two men bailing water out of a boat. and after this was done, passengers were transferred into it, while their boat went in search of other survivors. They had 85 people in their boat altogether. Many people slid down across the deck to the boats and she saw one little boy who was badly bruised for this reason. His mother, a native of Ireland, was rescued with him.

Another woman was flung into the water but managed to cling to a chair and was picked up. She went under water twice and described the pressure and the sensation of drowning as dreadful. One of the wireless operators who was in her boat said he sent out the SOS call for fourteen minutes. They could see boats coming out of Queenstown Harbour, and after a considerable time they were transferred to a pilot boat. They were well cared for at Queenstown. The people there she said gave up their rooms and did all they could for them. She lost all her belongings. It would be difficult to imagine from Mrs Anderson's pleasant chat that she has passed through such a terrible experience. She is possessed of strong nerves and a cheerful temperament and is supremely grateful for her narrow escape.'

In fact, Emily Anderson was to die within two years of the disaster, aged 28. When discussing the Anderson claim for compensation in Washington in February 1925, the board noted that Mrs Anderson's death was 'directly attributable to the injuries she received when the *Lusitania* was sunk'. In September 1915 Mrs Anderson gave birth to a son, Frank, but he was to die the following March – something that Barbara blames on the trauma her mother suffered in the aftermath of the disaster.

SAN JUAN
(1929)

5 March 2005

There was a real poignancy about the conversation I had tonight with Holis Pifer, a survivor of the *San Juan* disaster of 29 August 1929. Tomorrow is Mothers Day and 76 years ago Mr Pifer's mother died while saving his life. He was six years old.

The *San Juan* was a small ship that ran an overnight service from San Francisco to Los Angeles. It was inexpensive and what we today would call 'no frills'. Marjorie Pifer and her son Holis were visiting her parents in San Francisco and had taken the train up. For reasons that are clouded by time it was decided that, as a treat, Marjorie and her sisters would take the *San Juan* back to Los Angeles.

During the journey the *San Juan* collided with the tanker *S. C. T. Dodd*. It was a calm sea with a light breeze. As the *Dodd* pulled away from the *San Juan*'s hull, water rushed in. The *San Juan* sank in just three minutes. Amazingly, despite the rapidity of the sinking, there were 42 survivors – including little Holis.

HOLIS PIFER

66 It was late at night and we were in our cabin. The *San Juan* was rammed by a tanker. Mother rushed me up on deck and there was the tanker right beside us. Close enough for a sailor to say, 'Hand over the child. That ship's going to sink!' Mother passed me over the deck rail, saying, 'Take my son, I've got to go back for my sisters.'

The sailor sat me on the deck. From a sitting position I could see the *San Juan* quite clearly. It suddenly heeled over on her side and went down very quickly. Then she was gone. I was cold sat there on my own. I looked around and noticed that there were people on the deck above. I got up and found a ladder, which I climbed up to the next deck. A young woman – another survivor – embraced me and held on to me. The rest is a blank. Mother was a hero that night. Neither she nor her sisters survived.

Titanic threads...
William MacQuitty

And so this diary ends with the *Titanic*, just as it began. A few years ago I had an unexpected phone call from William MacQuitty who, as a little boy growing up in Belfast, had been taken to see the launching of the new White Star liner *Titanic*. I had written to Mr MacQuitty to say how much I admired his film version of the *Titanic* disaster – *A Night to Remember* – which he produced in the late 1950s. He had obviously got my number through directory enquiries as I hadn't enclosed it in my letter. I reiterated my enthusiasm for his film and in particular its documentary-style approach to the subject. Thinking back to that conversation today, it strikes me as foolish that I didn't ask him about seeing the real thing. I suppose I was rather in awe of his reputation and was rather taken aback that I was talking to him at all.

However, just recently I remembered that conversation and wondered if I should get in touch with him again so that I could interview him about the day in question. Alas, time has been my enemy. Today I found out that William MacQuitty passed away in February 2004. I very much wanted to include his recollection of the event in this diary so I went back to his publication *Titanic Memories: the making of A Night to Remember*. This is how he described watching the *Titanic* take to the water for the very first time:

'I was born in Belfast on 15 May 1905, which meant I was just past my sixth birthday when the *Titanic* was launched on 30 May 1911. The spectacle of her huge hull rising above the slipway at the Harland & Wolff shipyard as the work of the shipbuilders progressed had provided my childhood with one of its most vividly remembered sights. The *Titanic* was, as all Belfast and the rest of the world knew, going to be the largest, best-designed and most beautiful ship ever to sail the seas. It was beyond me, as a frail frightened little boy, plagued by asthma and bronchitis, to imagine how this huge mountain of metal could ever be floated, but my ancestors had provided me with my greatest asset: an enormous curiosity and persistence.

My father took me to the launch. The day was glorious and the sun shone from a clear sky. The smell of the sea mingled with the smells of the shipyard, where a vast throng of workers and spectators waited in awed silence. Suddenly a rocket flamed into the sky, the chocks were knocked away, hydraulic rams pushed and the huge vessel began to move down the slipway, very slowly at first, then faster and faster. It dragged the mounds of restraining anchor chains along the ground. A great wave rose as her stern hit the sea. The noise was thunderous. All the ships in Belfast harbour sounded their sirens, the vast crowd cheered, the hull was buoyed up by the water. My fears vanished. This great ship had been built by people like me. What they could do I would also be able to do in time. I too was an Ulsterman. My heart swelled with pride.

On 2 April the following year I saw the fitted-out *Titanic* as she sailed away to begin her maiden voyage. Before her lay the freedom of the oceans and I longed to be aboard. The news of her tragic fate twelve days later shocked the world. The inheritance of Victorian certainty was shattered and something had changed for ever. Worst hit were the people of Ulster, all of whom had links with the ship, through relatives, friends of the men who built her. It came as a dreadful shock to me as it did for everyone else, but I absorbed the basic lesson: time was the most precious gift of life, and death was for us all.'

He later adds:

'The original disaster certainly confirmed my belief that life is for the living as fully as possible. Lost opportunities do not return. "Too late" are the saddest words in any language. Time is our most precious gift.'

Now I shall close these pages on the past. It's been a fascinating voyage of discovery. Time well spent.

Bibliography and Acknowledgements

Books

Archbold, Rick and McCawley, Dana *Last Dinner on the Titanic* (Weidenfeld & Nicholson, 1997)

Bainbridge, Beryl *Every Man for Himself* (Abacus, 1996)

Ballard, Dr Robert D. *The Discovery of the Titanic* (Hodder & Stoughton, 1997) *Exploring the Lusitania* (Weidenfeld & Nicholson, 1995)

Beesley, Lawrence *The Loss of the Titanic* (Star, 1979; paperback reprint)

Bottomore, Stephen *The Titanic and Silent Cinema* (The Production Box, 2000)

Boyd-Smith, Jan and Peter *Southampton: Gateway to England* (Red Post Books, 2000)

Brittain, Vera *Testament of Youth* (1933; Virago, 1999)

Burton, Hal *The Morro Castle Tragedy at Sea* (Viking, 1973)

Cameron, James, annotated by Randal Frances *Titanic Illustrated Screenplay* (Boxtree, 1999)

Cameron, Stephen *Death in the North Channel: The Loss of the Princess Victoria, January 1953* (Colourpoint Books, 2003)

Coward, Noel *Autobiography* (Methuen, 1986)

Eaton, John P. and Haas, Charles A. *Titanic: Triumph and Tragedy: A Chronicle in words and pictures* (Patrick Stephens Ltd, 1986)

Forster, John Wilson (Ed) *Titanic* (Penguin, 1999)

Gallagher, Thomas *Fire at Sea: The story of the Morro Castle* (Muller, 1959)

Geller, Judith *Titanic: Women and Children First* (Patrick Stephens Ltd, 1998)

Green, Stanley *Broadway Musicals Show by Show* (Faber & Faber, 1985)

Hastings, Selina *Nancy Mitford* (Vintage, 2002)

Hoffer, William *Saved! The story of the Andrea Doria, the greatest sea rescue in history* (Macmillan, 1980)

Hutchinson, Gillian *The Wreck of the Titanic* (National Maritime Museum, 1994)

Hyslop, Donald, Forsyth, Alistair and Jemima, Sheila *Titanic Voices: Memories from the Fateful Voyage* (Sutton Publishing, 1998)

Lord, Walter *A Night to Remember* (1956; Illustrated Edition, Penguin Books, 1976) *The Night Lives On* (Viking, 1987)

Lynch, Don *Titanic: An Illustrated History* (Hodder & Stoughton/Madison Press Book, 1995)

MacQuitty, William *Titanic Memories: the Making of A Night to Remember* (National Maritime Museum, 2000)

Marchbanks, David *The Painted Ship* (Secker & Warburg, 1964)

159

Miller, William H. Jr *The Great Luxury Liners 1927-1954* (New York, Dover Publications Inc, 1981)
The Fabulous Interiors of the Great Ocean Liners in Historic Photographs (New York, Dover Publications Inc, 1985)
Moscow, Alvin *Collision Course* (Longmans, 1959)
Nolan, John *In Search of Great Uncle Pat* (Baltimore, America House, 2001)
O'Donnell, Edward T. *Ship Ablaze: The Tragedy of the Steamboat General Slocum* (New York, Broadway Books, 2003)
Stone, Peter *Titanic: The Complete Book of the Musical* (Applause Books, 1999)
Taylor, Irene and Alan (Ed) *The Assassin's Cloak: An Anthology Of The World's Greatest Diarists* (Canongate Books, 2003)
Thomas, Gordon and Witts, Max Morgan *Shipwreck: The Strange Fate of the Morro Castle* (Dell Publishing, 1972)
Wall, Robert *Ocean Liners* (London, Collins, 1978)
Williams, David *Wartime Disasters at Sea* (Patrick Stephens Ltd, 1995)
Watson, Milton H. *Disasters at Sea* (Patrick Stephens Ltd, 1987; 2nd ed updated and expanded by William H. Miller, 1995)

CD
Strauss, Richard (Translation Mari Prackauskas) *Vier Letzte Lieder*; Sir George Solti, Kiri Te Kanawa; Decca, 1991)

Journals
Atlantic Daily Bulletin Journal of The British Titanic Society (PO Box 401, Hope Carr Way, Leigh, Lancashire WN7 3WW

Website
Encyclopedia Titanica (http://www.encyclopedia-titanica.org)
Eastland Disaster Historical Society (info@eastlanddisaster.org)

The author would also like to thank the following people for their help:
First, my mum and dad for their continual encouragement.
Second, all of the survivors who agreed to speak to me – their patience and kindness is extraordinary.
In addition, the relatives and family friends of *Titanic* passengers who provided so much extra information.
Millvina Dean deserves a special mention because without her this diary would never have been written, a wonderful lady and a great friend.
Researchers Pat Cook, Shelley Dziedzic, Michael Findlay, Jim Kalafus (for his unending support, friendship and encyclopaedic knowledge of maritime disasters), Mike Poirier, Sean Szmalc, Brian Ticehurst and Ted Wachholz.
Finally, my dear friend and companion Leza Mitchell who has lived through the making of this diary almost as much as I have! We've had some interesting adventures... Thank you.